Every Life Should Have 9 Cats-

or more

(and maybe a dog)

Ida Riman Percoco
author of
LIMERICKS AND MINI-POEMS

SMALL WORLD
PUBLICATIONS
Orlando, Florida

*"He prayeth well who loveth well
Both man and bird and beast.*

*He prayeth best, who loveth best
All things both great and small;
For the dear God who loveth us,
He made and loveth all."*

Samuel Taylor Coleridge
<u>The Rime of the Ancient Mariner</u>

> For additional copies
> Send $13.95 per book
> plus 2.05 S&H to:
>   Ida Percoco
>   2420 Caribbean Court
>   Orlando, FL 32805

Copyright © 2001 Ida Riman Percoco
All Rights Reserved

No part of this book may be reproduced or transmitted in any form or by any means, electronic, mechanical, including photocopying, recording, or by any information storage and retrieval system, except in the case of reviews, without the express written permission of the publisher, except where permitted by law.

Library of Congress Catalog Number   01-135768

ISBN Number   1-57087-589-8

Printed in the United States of America

FOREWORD

Here are the stories and poems about some of our cats and our dog. Many are histories. Others are observations on their activities while they are interacting—just being themselves. Some are what I call "generic," about cats and dogs in general.

We adopted a street kitten, whom we named Mitzi, in 1953, And since then, we have had a cat, or a number of cats, ending in year 2000, with nine. And, for 15 years, we were lucky to have the friendship and companionship of our dog. He left us in 1997.

During the 47 years, our pets have frolicked, loved, and given us happy years and sad ones. They age or become sick, and eventually, they cross the "rainbow bridge." Sometimes we have to help them. We concentrate on the happy memories.

I have read many books about animal communication and animal passing. I am convinced that life, in some form, goes on—not only for people, but for our four-legged friends. So, with our grief at losing a pet, we are consoled by that belief. And we can give our love and attention to those who remain with us.

We keep the garage cats separate because cats don't accept strange felines peaceably. And we don't want raging battles. One of my stories is about what happened when we put an outside cat into the back enclosure.

If you are fortunate enough to have the friendship of companion animals, you will relate to the experiences of our pets. If you are not, you may gain a deeper understanding of their actions and their lives, Always bear in mind, that animals, although they can be conditioned, act by instinct. And that each species has, for its survival, a complex set of built-in movements and reactions. However, within their limitations, all are individuals, each with his own personality and sense of self.

Ida Riman Percoco

ACKNOWLEDGMENTS

I appreciate the help and inspiration given me by my friends at the Beardall Center, Orlando, Florida, writing workshop. Their input has been invaluable. I am afraid to list their names. If I inadvertently leave someone out, I will never forgive myself. But I thank them one and all.

I want to thank Karen Weinberg of MODesign in Winter Park, Florida, for her expertise with the computer. She put up with the confusion of getting this book together and the idiosyncrasies of the author.

I especially want to give credit to the late Cleveland Amory whose kindness and encouragement resulted in the publication of my work. Mr. Amory was kind, not only to animals, but to people. I cherish his letters and his memory.

And of course, I dedicate this work to the person whose unfailing love and support made it all possible--my husband, Joseph Percoco.

Ida Riman Percoco
Orlando, Florida, 2001

COVER ART BY

Melanie Mauery
Coastline Studios
Orlando, Florida

TABLE OF CONTENTS

FROM THE BEGINNING

FROM THE BEGINNING 1952-1964 (We adopt our first cats) 1
WILLY 7

THE CENTRAL ISLIP YEARS

INTRODUCTION, THE CENTRAL ISLIP YEARS 9
ALMOST A DOG 12
NANCY AND BLACKIE 13
TIMMY 14
SHERRY 16
GREENER GRASS 16

THE ORLANDO YEARS

INTRODUCTION, THE ORLANDO YEARS 17
EQUAL BUT SEPARATE 19
ON THE DEATH OF CURLY (A favorite pet) 20
NOBODY'S DOG 21
DAILY ROUTINE 21
LONESOME 22
FELINE CHOW TIME 26
ANYBODY WANT A DOG? 27
OLD CAT SYLVIE 28
GONE 29
CANDY 30
INDIVIDUALS 34
CONFRONTATION AT THE "C" CORRAL 37
JINNY JOINS US 39
JINNY 42
THE YOUNG AND THE AGELESS 43
SAY "CHEESE" 44
JERRY'S MORNING 46
CHOW TIME 48
LONESOME AND THE VISITOR 49
BLACKIE 50
CAT JERRY 51
FUN AND GAMES 52

Table of Contents (continued)

JAMIE	*53*
UNIQUE(Johnny)	*57*
WOOGA-WOOGA	*58*
HE-ERE'S JOHNNY!	*60*
RUSTY AND LONESOME	*63*
CAT CIRCUS	*66*
THE EIGHT THAT WALK	*71*
FURRY FUN	*73*
TAMING BLONDIE	*74*
JINNY'S DAY	*75*
A TALE OF CLAWS	*76*
QUINTET	*78*
CANINE COMMUNICATION	*79*
MITTY SPEAKS	*80*
EXIT WHITEY	*81*
WALKING OUR DOG ON AN EARLY SPRING MORNING	*83*
JINNY'S QUANDARY	*84*
THE GARAGE CATS AND THE MILK	*85*
SPAT	*85*
SICK CAT	*86*
FAREWELL, LONESOME	*88*
WATCHING MITTY	*91*
MITTY'S ORDEAL	*92*
INSTINCTS	*94*
MITTY'S DILEMMA	*95*
ANOTHER CAT TALE	*96*
BLONDIE OUTSIDE	*98*

THE NINE CATS

BLONDIE AND THE CARS	*101*
BLONDIE AND FRIEND	*102*
BEWILDERED MITTY	*102*
RANDY'S TOY	*103*
THE INSPECTOR	*104*

Table of Contents (continued)

ET CETERA
(And Others of the Like Kind)

DOGGONE IT	105
DOG DAYS	105
THE DIVINE ESSENCE	105
VISIT TO THE VET	106
CAT CHRISTMAS	107
SCAREDY CAT	108
THE FELINE	108
NO JUSTICE	109
FRED AND WILLIE	110
TO A CAT	111
WHY DO I LOVE YOU?	112
SEPARATE AND UNEQUAL	113
WILD KITTEN ADOPTED	114
TIPPED SCALES	115
BIBLIOGRAPHY (Books with evidence of animal survival)	116
INDEX OF TITLES	117
INDEX OF FIRST LINES, POEMS	119
ABOUT THE AUTHOR	120

FROM THE BEGINNING

FROM THE BEGINNING

Alvie

Desdemona

Freddie

Mickey

Mitzi

Patty

Penny

Susie

Willy

FROM THE BEGINNING
1952-1964
(We adopt our first cats)

Joe and I were married in 1952. We bought a little two-bedroom, one-bath attached home in Flushing, New York. One day, stopping at a commercial site off a busy street, we were accosted by a grey mottled female kitten. When she headed toward the road, we picked her up and looked for some indication of where she had come from. We saw only a parking lot and a building—it might have been a used-car business—no sign of a house or anyone who expressed interest in the little animal. We decided to take her home—our first cat.

We called her Mitzi. We left her in the house while we both went to work, giving her a litter box in our finished basement. In the evenings and weekends she played outside. She followed me in the garden, running and dancing for the sheer joy of being alive. When I dug a hole to plant something, she helped me, alternating paws as she vigorously clawed out soil.

When we came home from work and I saw her pawprints on the stove or table, I spanked her. A new cat owner, I was ignorant of the fact that she could not relate the punishment to the deed. One evening, when we came home and I approached her, I saw her trembling. That was the end of the "training" sessions.

Mitzi became pregnant before we realized that she could conceive. She was still a kitten. She had a small litter. The two offspring died. The next-door neighbor to the right of our attached home, owned a cat who also had a litter when Mitzi's were born. That cat's young died also. Mrs. Kelly thought that the father probably had defective genes. We realized that Mitzi would have to be spayed. I don't remember the name of the vet or the details of the spaying, but Mitzi survived and thrived.

One evening we happened to be looking out of our front window and saw that Mitzi had been picked up by a boy about fourteen or fifteen years old. He held her, carrying her away from the house. Joe ran out. "Put down that cat," he commanded. The teen dropped Mitzi. Somehow, I thought I glimpsed a strange expression on his face, a veiled threat. But he said nothing. I worried.

Less than a week later, one of our neighboring girls, also in her teens, came to tell us that Mitzi was dead. Our cat had been hit by a car and was on the road that ran at right angles to our street. We went to get her. Her head had been flattened by the vehicle. It was too sudden to be a coincidence. We remembered the look on the face of the boy who had carried her. We could prove nothing, could do nothing. We buried Mitzi in the field beyond our dead end street. And some of the joy went out of our lives.

The same girl who had given us the news of Mitzi's death came to our house a few days later. There was a stray kitten running around the neighborhood. Some boys had been swinging her by the tail. She would not last long if she was not given a home. And no one wanted her. Still desolate without Mitzi, we decided to take this kitten. Because of her rust-colored coat, we called her Penny.

Penny, a street-wise animal, avoided the children and hid from all strangers. Although not too friendly, she allowed us to pet her. For a short time, she shared our house in Flushing.

At the same time that we adopted Penny, Joe's sister Mary, living at the family home, also in Flushing, decided to buy a pure-bred kitten, choosing a Siamese. She brought home a noisy little male, tan, not yet deeply colored, with turquoise eyes. He was a mild little fellow, and the family loved him. Mary called him BeBop, ignoring his pedigree and string of non-English monikers. An inside cat, he could not be allowed to roam in apartment-house neighborhoods with busy streets. Someone might have stolen him, or he might have been hit by a car.

Then BeBop's loud wail began to irritate Joe's mother, a semi-invalid. So BeBop had to go. When Mary asked us if we would take him, we agreed on a trade—BeBop for Penny. So Penny went to the family, BeBop to us. We renamed him Freddie.

Because Penny was a grouch, Joe's father loved to tease her and hear her hiss and growl. They let her out. Penny stayed away from people and avoided cars. She scooted across busy Kissena Boulevard when she saw a break in traffic and went hunting in the then-undeveloped property on the opposite side of the highway. She had not yet been spayed, but there were no male cats in the area. Eventually, she had the surgery.

Freddie, at our house, was a quiet animal, completely different from our previous two cats. Our property was more isolated than that of Joe's parents, so we did let him out in the evening, He found another male cat and the two chased each other in the field that ended our street. Accidentally, we discovered that Freddie loved raw fish. So that became his diet—raw frozen fish that he ate with relish as it thawed. We knew nothing about nutrition at that time—neither for people nor animals. We didn't realize then, but we know now, that while we were feeding Freddie all he wanted to eat, he was dying of malnutrition. It had to happen.

Our left-side neighbor came to us. "Your cat is dead. He is in the path in the field."

We ran out and picked up his still-warm body. Not a mark on him. Frantically, we looked for a vet. None were available; too late, anyway. We buried Freddie near Mitzi. And we learned a valuable lesson. No more raw fish for the animals.

Willy, short for Wilbur, became our next pet. This all black, except for a white key on his neck, kitten appeared from nowhere, afraid of everything and everyone. The same male that had been Freddie's pal became Willy's enemy. When we heard our kitten screaming we ran out and chased the other cat. Willy reached adulthood and was neutered. And, when we bought a Dairy Queen, still in the 1950's, and moved to West Milford, New Jersey, he came with us. He began a new life. We found a few dead chipmunks and water rats. They abounded in our lake community. After two hectic summers, Joe and I tired of the Dairy Queen and the work load it entailed, rented it out, and returned to our previous technical illustrating field. (Eventually, we rid ourselves of the Dairy Queen when the county removed the building and put a road through the lot on which it had stood. They reimbursed us for the building and equipment, not the business.)

For a short time we worked at a company in downtown New York City, driving to a parking lot on the New Jersey side of the Hudson river and taking a bus into the city. When that ended we decided to job shop, doing temporary work where needed.

One of our assignments took us to Norden in Norwalk, Connecticut. It was one hundred miles each way, high speed driving. We crossed the Tappan Zee Bridge just as the sky turned a pale pink on the horizon. And then rode on the Connecticut Turnpike to Norwalk. So much stress resulted from this trip that we stayed at a motel in Norwalk every other day.

Poor Willy!. At first, we tried to lock him in the house with food and water and a litter box. But he became so frantic when we came home that we left him outside and fed him when we returned every other day.

Our stint at Norden lasted a little over a month. It was profitable. We had a good hourly rate and received a per diem because the job was so far from home. Between that and the rent we received from the Dairy Queen we would have been able to save some money. After that ended, we had a short assignment at Grumman in Bethpage, New York. What a trip! Through the Lincoln Tunnel, through New York City, and on the Long Island Expressway and back. That job ended soon, and we free-lanced, taking work and doing it at home.

One day, in front of our house, I found a kitten. One of its eyes was runny. By this time, I had discovered neighbors who had seven or eight cats. I had never known anyone who owned more than one or two. They kept the animals in the house. Because they could not afford to spay the females, they had the males neutered and put up with the aggravation of the females in heat. Charlie and Ade were in their eighties, two of the nicest people I have ever known. Ade—she asked me to call her "Ade"—followed pregnant feral cats in the area—summer people went back to the city and abandoned their pets—and drowned the litters as soon as they were born. She cried when she did it, but she knew that allowing wild cats to proliferate would cause suffering to starving animals without winter shelter, and also wildlife.

Charlie and Ade would, I was certain, take the kitten with the bleary eye. What was one more cat to people who had that many. I called Ade and she came over. "Poor little thing," she said, "it probably has a bad cold in the eye." She came daily for over a week, ministering to the tiny animal, bathing the eye. We discovered that the kitten was a female.

"What can I do?" I whined. "I wonder who will give her a home? Is there a humane society anywhere near here?"

Ade looked at me strangely. "It is a blessing to befriend a little kitten like this" she said. "She will keep your other cat company."

That was that. For the first time, we had more than one pet. We called the grey-striped kitten Susie, or "Little Sus." Ade found out what had happened to her. A neighbor down the road, who fed some of the abandoned ferals, had found Little Sus hanging from her fence, a beebee in one eye. The lady took the kitten down, removed the beebee and, in her front yard, started to treat the eye. Then the phone rang. She went in to answer it. When she returned the kitten had disappeared. "My heart bled for that little thing," she told us when we met her a few weeks later.

My sister lived in Monroe, New York, at the time, just a few miles north of our home in West Wilford. On a visit, somehow we took Little Sus with us. Sarah saw that the kitten was flea-infested and gave me some flea powder. After rubbing it into the kitten's fur, the fleas began to fall off, dead. I counted more than 50. They had been eating Susie alive. When we returned home, I continued the boric acid for the eye and the flea treatments. Obviously, she would never see out of the bad eye. But she thrived and gained weight. Ade came over to see her once in a while.

We found a farm vet in New York State, just over the New Jersey border. He decided that, because of Susie's trauma, it would be better to wait before spaying. Eventually, she went into heat. Fortunately, there were no male cats in the vicinity. And when her estrus subsided, we took her for the surgery. Joe and I will never forget going back to the vet to pick her up. As soon as we entered the reception room and said a few words, there burst upon our ears a loud and pathetic meowing from the back room. "It's your cat," said the vet. "She knows you. She's a little devil," he continued. "She pulled out her stitches. I had to reclose the incision with stainless steel wire." We took Little Sus home. A week later the stitches were removed. She made a fine recovery.

Some time after that, a long-haired male cat appeared behind our house, befriending both Susie and Willy. I fed him, but I was sure he belonged to someone. He was tan and white, peaches and cream, with extra toes on his front paws. He was amiable and purred when petted. Surely someone had loved him. Perhaps, being male, he had wandered off, looking for a mate. Once again, I called Ade. She asked everyone she knew—and she knew almost everyone—if any of the year-round residents had lost a cat. No one had. So—Joe and I had another cat. My sister had told me about a friend's cat, long-haired and blonde, named Alvin. Well, this was another Alvin, Alvin the second. We called him Alvie. Now we had three felines.

In Flushing, Joe's sister Mary, had married and left home. Joe's mother now couldn't stand Penny's meowing, and Joe's father couldn't take care of the cat. Would we take her back? So we brought Penny to New Jersey. Four cats; we were getting there. Penny had been a hunter all her life, She went to our lake and caught water rats. She ate what she killed. Little Sus also visited the lake, eating small fish that had washed up on shore.

One day, when I crossed the street to talk with a neighbor, Little Sus followed me. She stationed herself at the foot of the steps leading to the door, meowing furiously until I came out. "She is worried about me," I told my friend who replied, "I never came across anything like that." I never did, either.

Susie followed me home. She always came with me when I went into our back property to garden or spray the poison ivy. She sat on my shoulder as I worked, a sweet little animal, miraculously rescued from a bitter fate.

Susie lived two years, A passing car side-swiped her. I found her stiff in the front yard a few feet from the road. She had been a favorite and we had loved her. We would never forget her.

Penny, always on her own, came back to the house with one eye closed. We took her to the vet. Her eye, he told us, would be permanently sightless. The vet didn't know how the eye had been damaged. Losing one eye didn't seem to bother Penny. She continued her journeys to the lake, hunting as before.

My sister had now moved from Monroe to Long Island in the Suffolk County village of Setauket. Her husband had been offered a position at the Brookhaven Center. On one of our visits, Sarah told us about an abandoned mother cat with two kittens on a deserted road. We said, "all right, we'll take one kitten." That would bring our menagerie back to four cats.

Daylight had faded when Sarah drove us down that road. In the beams of the headlights we saw the mother with two grey kittens. We decided on the one we wanted, picked it up, and went back to the car. Then we turned around. There, blinking in the light, sat the little mother and the other kitten. "I don't know what will happen to them," Sarah said. "That road goes to a farm. The mother can probably fend for herself but the kitten won't survive." We went back, picked up the mother and the other kitten. The three went back to New Jersey with us. We named the mother cat Desdemona after Cicero's cat. We called her "Desi." Her two male kittens became Pat and Mike, "Patty and Mickey."

We lived in West Milford five years. During that time we increased our population from one cat to six. When, after the dismantling of the Dairy Queen, we decided to move back to New York, buying a new house in a new subdivision in Central Islip (now renamed Islandia), we brought them all with us—Willy, Alvie, Penny, Desi, Patty, and Mickey.

1957

WILLY

Willy's wobbly head makes him a pathetic little animal, especially on rainy days. With his lack of balance, he can't even hop onto his favorite tail-chasing chair without a struggle Sometimes, I think he says, "On your mark, get set—" When he finally jumps, it is a fumbling jump. He barely makes it. His feet all claw in the air—one or two paws catch the chair, and he pulls himself up. When he is up, he seems so relieved. He lies on the seat and curls his forepaws over the edge, gripping and purring. When watched and spoken to kindly, he goes through a kneading motion over the edge of the chair seat. Or he puts his forepaws together, elbows akimbo and looks for all the world like a child's rubber duck about to bob on the ripples in the tub.

His tail-chasing on his favorite chair is a never-ending source of entertainment to us and diversion for him. Only on that chair does the tail get chased. Wherever we put the chair, he finds it. Round and round he goes, sometimes managing to hold on to the tail for a second. Then, dizzy and off-balance, he chases it off the chair, winding up on the floor. The poor animal is bewildered for a moment. Then he gets back on the chair with determination, and the chase begins again. After five or six on-off's, Willy gives up and comes to us, nagging for food or attention. Or he climbs on the armchair into his crocheted catnapper. Then he snoozes.

Now and then Joe feels that Willy's efforts to snare the tail should be rewarded. So Joe takes the tall and holds it in place. Then poor Willy licks and chews at it vigorously for a while. Or, mistaking the human's intentions, he bites the hand that holds the tail, but never with intent to injure. He is such a good little animal.

THE CENTRAL ISLIP YEARS

THE CENTRAL ISLIP YEARS

Sooty & Dusty

Dusty

Curly

Sandy

Teddy

Timmy

Sylvie

THE CENTRAL ISLIP YEARS

Candy

Betsy

Buddy & Franzie

Sherry

Nancy

Tommy

Spooky

INTRODUCTION, THE CENTRAL ISLIP YEARS

We moved from West Milford, New Jersey, to Central Islip, New York, in 1964–and from Central Islip to Orlando, Florida, in 1978. When we left West Milford, we had six cats. We came to Orlando, bringing eight. Not the same ones. Time has a way of changing relationships.

Willy and Patty disappeared. Desdemona (Desi or Momsy), Mickey, and Penny "crossed the rainbow bridge," due to illness or old age, assisted by a veterinarian. My sister fell in love with Alvie, the long-haired pale orange male. We hated to part with him, but yielded to her pleading. Alvie lived a long life and finally had to be helped escape the problems of time.

People in Central Islip (we called it "CI") saw a number of cats near our house. They assumed we operated an animal shelter. Cats appeared from nowhere and ended up in our yard. The doorbell would ring and, upon opening the door, a box of kittens greeted our eyes. We advertised them for adoption, brought some to a non-kill shelter (after a while, the shelter refused to take any more unless they were especially adoptable), and kept some.

Ginger, a pretty orange female, shared our home for a few years. Blackie, a feral, lost his life to urine blockage. Franzie–brother of Fonzie who was adopted–had a genetic illness like his littermate. Both died. We found homes also for the other two kittens from the litter. Debbie, a pretty long-haired tortoiseshell, was adopted immediately; then returned to us when the elderly owners became ill. A no-kill shelter took her–we had had her spayed–and found a home for her. Timmy, an orange long-haired male, Alvie's look-alike, stayed with us for a short time, until hemo botanella claimed him. Leo disappeared. Eddy and Terry had to be put down–both too hard to live with, Bobby, my mother's cat, given to us when she became unable to take care of him, disappeared. Spooky, a pretty black-and-white female, had eye problems which resulted in the removal of a badly-swollen blind eye; she later died of other problems. Sherry, two years old, surrendered to feline leukemia.

Nancy, a pretty little orange cat, gave us her friendship for a short period; then died of an unknown (to the vet) illness. From Sandy, an extremely friendly peaches-and-cream male, we removed a beebee which had barely missed a vital spot. To save his life, my sister took him; he disappeared after less than a week at her house. With the University of Stonybrook and its laboratories so close, we suspected the worst.

The cat who remains most strongly in our memories was Teddy. This stray, at first thin and bony, came to our house for a kind word and food. We called him "gray boy." After a while, we decided to give him a permanent name– "Teddy," since he reminded us of a teddy bear. One day, he seemed barely able to crawl to our house. We took him to a veterinarian, The vet examined him. Someone had beaten the cat and broken the tail, which dangled lifelessly. He also had internal injuries. The doctor took a fancy to Teddy. We asked if the man would like to adopt the cat. No, but he would like to help. First, the tail had to be amputated. Then various medication would have to be given to help heal the cat internally,

After we took Teddy home, we put him in a makeshift enclosure we had created out of chicken wire against our side fence. The poor animal sat on a redwood bench in the enclosure and howled in pain. It was hard to bear. Time went by, and the anus healed. But, without the tail, it was exposed to whatever was in the air. And the poor cat had no control over his eliminations or his wetting. As a matter of fact, for a while he had no eliminations. We took him back to the vet, asking the man to euthanize him. Instead the vet used some suppositories to induce an elimination.

"The cat is too nice to put down. He has suffered. Let him live." So we let Teddy live.

We had to pad with newspaper, the furniture in the family room and the radiators on which the cats liked to sleep. And after Teddy lay on them, we had to wrap up the wet paper and the stool for garbage pickup. Of course, Teddy also was wet and dirty, I wiped his fur with a damp paper towel. He purred. I was near tears.

For six years Teddy lived with us. In the summer flies followed him, drawing blood from his exposed anus. I sponged the area when he came into the house. He purred with pleasure. Just before we moved to Orlando, I discovered that the area harbored maggots.

Horrified, Joe and I took Teddy to a vet, not the one who had originally treated him. This doctor took one look and said, "How could you let an animal go around like that? The only thing to do is put him down. He is in misery. And it would even be worse in Orlando."

We loved Teddy. His acceptance of his problems, his pain, went to our hearts, How could anyone be so cruel as to hurt a helpless animal? We never will understand it. We left his remains in CI. A few weeks later we moved to Orlando.

These cats moved with us–Tommy, a black and white male who came to us as a stray kitten; Dusty, an all-gray male whom I adopted through an ad in the paper; Sylvie, an abandoned tortoiseshell female; Buddy, the veterinary donor cat for Timmy when Timmy needed blood, a handsome gray-and-white male tabby with a white chest and mask; Sooty, an all-black stray tomcat, scarred from fighting, whom we had fed in CI; Candy, a sweet female calico; Curly, a male, named for his curly tail, one of an abandoned litter which had also contained Sherry; and Betsy, a chunky little grey female with a white chest, paws, and mask, who came, pregnant, in our yard, bleeding in the armpit from a paw caught in a loose collar.

Eight cats–we were still one short of nine.

1970

ALMOST A DOG

On my way home from a shopping trip, driving along a seldom-used side street, I spotted a dog lying in the center of the road.

I came closer, but the dog didn't get up.

"Poor thing," I thought, "perhaps it is hurt."

I stopped the car, opened the door, and went out to look more closely at the animal. As I did so, it stood up, ran to the car, and jumped in. I saw that he was male, a medium-size brownish mixed-breed.

How to get him out? Coaxing was to no avail. Perhaps someone had lost him, At any rate, since I couldn't get him out of the car, I decided to take him home and advertise for his owner.

Home we went. I offered some food. The dog ate.

The canine seemed to get along with our felines, He was docile, and allowed us to pet him–stroking that we did gently, as his skin seemed to be wet. Joe looked him over closely–a collar, but no tag, bad skin, thin.

"Let's take him to the vet," my husband said. "Perhaps the vet might be able to help us find the owner."

The dog went into our car willingly, seemed to enjoy the ride, and sat quietly in the vet's waiting room,

The doctor examined him. "This dog has so many things wrong it's hardly worth treating him. He was probably abandoned. The best thing you could do would be to have him put down."

We felt sorry for the animal.

"No," disagreed Joe. "Save him."

"If that's what you want, okay."

The vet treated the dog for mange, worms, and whatever else could be diagnosed; then sent our patient home with a corrugated box holding at least ten medications. In return, we left a sizeable amount of cash–totaling over a hundred dollars. Oh, well, the animal was worth saving. We felt smug about doing a good deed.

We bought some dog food. He had little appetite. Our entry foyer became the dog's apartment for the night. In the morning, we discovered a mess. He had eliminated and wet. So we shoveled and wiped.

During the day, he could stay in our fenced back yard.

All he needed would be a bowl of water. And, at night, he'd get the food and medication.

Joe led the pooch into the fenced area and locked the gate; then went to work.

Later that morning, I went out to see how the dog was doing.

He was nowhere to be found. Evidently he had jumped the four-foot fence and taken off.

We now had a box of medication but no patient. We discussed what had possibly created the events that had just taken place.

We thought the dog had come to stay with us. Instead, he had been abandoned or lost and was looking for his family. He probably used my car to hitchhike in the direction he thought I would take him. Perhaps home was now closer. And, a little less hungry and a little less sick, someone's pet continued his journey.

As for us, we almost had a dog.

1971

NANCY AND BLACKIE

Big cat Blackie was curled up and sleeping;
Little Nan looked and came to him, creeping.
Blackie opened his eyes, yawned to greet her,
And with all of his paws, stretched to meet her.

Nancy rubbed on his head, began licking;
It was time, Blackie thought, to start kicking.
Little Nan jumped away quite dejected;
Her reception was not as expected.

"I don't mind," Blackie said, "if you're creepy.
But don't bother me when I'm sleepy."

1976

TIMMY

The neighborhood adored him,
  The long-haired scrawny stray.
None knew where he had come from,
  But he was here to stay.

Behind my house he wandered—
  Through my glass door he stared.
His face was grey and haggard
  (Although the whole street cared).

I wondered if they fed him—
  I put some food outside.
He cleaned the dish and looked up,
  With eyes not scared, but wide.

I gave him food another time;
  Once more he cleaned the plate.
I opened then the door and called;
  The cat came in and ate.

He ate, he drank, he gorged himself,
  And then he fell asleep.
I petted him, and I was shocked—
  Just bones and knots, a heap.

I sheared away his knotted fur;
  I fed him every day.
A few weeks passed; his fur came clean,
  And he began to play.

I could not find a home for him;
  I asked each girl and boy.
They loved him just to fondle him;
  They thought he was a toy.

I put him with our other cats,
  And he became our pride.
He lived with us about a year,
  And then our Timmy died.

He was so good and beautiful,
  Admired by all who knew-
So lovable and love-giving,
  Unique among a few.

If animals should have a soul,
  As many psychics say,
My soul will meet with Timmy's soul,
  And he and I will play.

He'll put his paws up to be raised
  And nuzzle on my cheek,
And purr and softly look at me.
  What need had he to speak?

When Timmy left us, we were sad,
  But somehow couldn't cry.
Subconsciously, we understood
  His soul will never die.

1977

SHERRY

He was Shere Khan, my baby cat—Sherry;
A little tiger, partly gray, partly black, partly brown.
He was my little brown cat.
He was Poppin' Fresh, Popsy, Popsicle, Shericle.
He was little Tweet, my little Tweet.
He followed me and rolled on his side
To be petted—and gently poked—Poppin' Fresh.
His big eyes begged patiently to be lifted to my lap.
He purred softly and kneaded hard.
He was alert, but toward the end he slept a lot
And ate little,
His pigeon-toed hoppy run became a walk—slow.
        He had lymphatic leukemia.
Poor little brown cat—
Hardly older than a kitten.
I don't understand it.

1977

GREENER GRASS

When you are inside the house,
You are always at the door,
Waiting for my sleight-of-hand
To come and set you free.

When you are outside the house,
You are always at the door,
Waiting for my magic touch
To come and let you in.

Little cat with human traits,
You are yearning to find out
What there is beyond the door,
What is on the other side.

THE ORLANDO YEARS

THE ORLANDO YEARS

Nicky

Felicia

Garage Cats -
Clockwise from top:
Whitey, Brandy, Blondie,
Sandy, & Rusty

Blackie & Inky

Mitty & Johnny

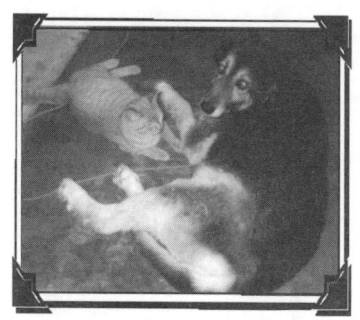

Rusty & Lonesome

HOUSE LAYOUT

Canal

| Computer Room | Fla Room | Back Enclosure Cat Corral |

House

Side Enclosure Cat Corral

Porch

Garage

Road

Enclosures

Back

Side

INTRODUCTION, THE ORLANDO YEARS

When we arrived in Orlando, with the eight cats in four aircraft-approved pet carriers, we gave them our Florida room for the night, They had the water, food and litter box, those three basic necessities.

We had learned a lesson from our experiences in CI. Cats who are allowed to roam often meet with disaster. Our makeshift chicken wire enclosure had not been able to keep them safe. They could climb the fence, claw the wire and, upside down, chin over the exposed edge of the mesh. We determined to have a professionally-built enclosure to house the felines.

Before the enclosure was put up, we lost Buddy. Someone had hit him, opening up a gash in his hind leg. The vet treated the gash, but the cat acquired feline infectious peritonitis from another patient in the animal clinic. It proved fatal.

And, after the enclosure had been built, we yielded to Sooty's demands to be free. After all, we thought, the black male was street-wise. He knew enough to be afraid of people. However, he didn't know enough to stay out of our neighbor's vegetable garden. She killed him.

A fence company put up the enclosure, chain link on two sides (the other two sides are the back of the house and the Florida room). It measures 10 feet by 37 feet, high enough so that a six-footer can stand straight on tiptoes. And the chain link connects the vertical fencing with the roof of the house. In it we have bushes and grass. Joe built a "gym," three vertical 4 x 4's, set at right angles, connected at various heights by 2 x 4 planks. At a number of locations on the fence, I attached "swings," short boards offering "windowsill" viewing areas.

We bought a pet-port, cut an opening through the door from the Florida room, and installed the animal entrance. They had had a pet port in CI and knew how to use one. That door is the only entrance to the enclosure.

One of the advantages of this arrangement soon became apparent. If we had to travel for a few days, a neighbor could enter the Florida room through the sliding glass doors which lead to the back yard and give the cats food and water. The cats would be there when we came home.

With the enclosure, which we call the "cat corral," we had a number of cats come and go. In addition to the original eight, we offered a temporary home to Inky, Blackie II, Nicky (who lived only a few months), and Felicia. Those 12 crossed the rainbow bridge during the years, leaving the five who are now in the Florida room and the back corral–Jinny, Jerry, Jamie, Johnny, and Mitty.

When we adopted an additional five in 1993, knowing that the first felines would reject the newcomers, we called the fence company to build another enclosure, this one at the side of the house, accessible through the back garage door, with the addition of a pet port. Again, Joe built a "gym," and I added viewing planks to the chain link at various heights. The second enclosure, measuring 7-1/2 feet by 28 feet and the same height as the first, likewise offers grass and bushes.

The last five, our "garage cats," were given the entire garage as their home. And they also have the advantage of their outside corral.

They should have been safe, but as my story, "The Eight That Walk," reveals, we still had not learned our lesson. And we lost Whitey. In the year 2000, the garage and the enclosure are shared by Rusty, Sandy, Randy and Blondie.

Nine cats.

1981

EQUAL BUT SEPARATE

Animals are all unique, though lion, dog, or mouse;
For instance, seven felines who reside within our house

Tommy, the philosopher, who takes things in his stride;
Timid little Candy who is quick to run and hide;

Feisty, loudmouth Betsy who gives all the rest a shot;
Pretty, patient Sylvie eats when they vacate a spot;

Sooty, the suspicious one, prepared to turn and run;
Blackie, noisy, friendly, always on the search for fun;

Dusty, widely talking with a voice I hardly hear;
Each an individual within his bounded sphere—

Each with his own sense of self, his dignity and pride,
All within the limits of a species, classified.

1981

ON THE DEATH OF CURLY
(A favorite pet)

Why did you die, my little cat,
Who sat upon my knee
And gave his love and trust to one-
His special person, me?

Why did you go, my little one?
You were too young to leave;
I hold within my useless tears,
While silently, I grieve.

Why did you die, my little cat-
Was I at fault somehow?
Could I have saved you, little friend-
What good to question now?

Why did you go, my little Curl?
The years will dull the pain;
But still the scar, my furry friend,
Forever will remain.

1982

NOBODY'S DOG

You shared our lives a few short weeks-
A timid, peaceful dog with mournful eyes.
Did someone give you food, perhaps not quite enough?
You searched for tidbits from torn garbage bags.
You made a mess, and there were murmurs, there were threats.

Did someone love you once as you were growing up?
Did someone hit you, hurt you, timid dog?
Did someone push you from a car
Into a strangeness that you could not comprehend?

You couldn't answer were you here. You disappeared.
Did someone carry out those threats, sweet timid dog?
We don't know whence you came;
we don't know where you've gone.

* * *

Note: he did return and became our dog, Lonesome.

1985

DAILY ROUTINE

"Come on, Sylvie, time to eat,
Come on, lady, move your feet.
Don't just stretch and yawn and rub;
Food is waiting—get your grub.

"Door is open, open wide;
Move it, Sylvie, come inside,
Come on, girl, enough's enough—
Door is closing—no food. Tough!"

Woman smart, but feline win;
I go out to bring her in.

1985

LONESOME

Every now and then, in our community, a dog or cat appears out of nowhere. It scrounges around for food, going from door to door, breaking into garbage bags. It plays with the children. Then it disappears, Sometimes a resident takes it to the humane society. Sometimes animal control is called. Sometimes—rarely—it finds a home with a kind-hearted family. A cat is more likely to find a home than a dog. But once in a while, a dog is lucky. Such a dog was Lonesome.

We don't know when someone abandoned him. But, after we saw the animal a number of times, associating with the dog of a neighbor who lived across the street, we suspected that he had been dropped off. We would see the now-stray for a week or so; then he would vanish, to return again on our street after a few days.

What the dog ate we didn't know. It might have been the food put out for the neighbor's pet. We knew the homeless animal broke into garbage bags. A few times I offered him some of the dry food I bought for our cats. The canine kept at a distance, but when I retreated, sniffed the crunchies. He didn't eat them. One day I laid a slice of bread on the lawn. To my surprise, the stray ate the bread. After that, whenever he came near the house, I offered bread. Eventually, he became bold enough to accept it from my hand.

He was a big dog, mostly shepherd—about half black, with tan around eyes, muzzle, paws; tan on stomach, skirt, and plumy tail. The hair around his neck was matted and dirty. Something about the eyes held me. There was a depth of loneliness and sadness in those eyes. I called him "Lonesome."

I jog in the morning and become a little apprehensive when I run past a dog. Eventually, I learned that my neighbor's old dog wouldn't attack me. But here was a large predator. At first, I slowed to a walk, passing him. Lonesome looked at me with sad eyes, but didn't run after me. After a few weeks, I worked up enough courage to jog past him. He didn't bark or make an attempt to chase me. Gradually, I lost my fear.

After a few weeks of jogging past him, the dog began to follow me. He didn't run, didn't get close, but stalked at a safe distance. We jogged together—"separate, but equal." If I went down the street to talk with a neighbor, Lonesome accompanied me, waiting patiently until I came out of the house, and then following me home.

The abandoned animal began to sleep behind the azalea bushes in front of our house, obviously feeling safe there because we didn't chase him. He dug trenches and slept in them. Annoyed, I filled in the holes and covered them with boards. The dog still slept behind the plants, but on the boards. Periodically he left, sometimes for a week or so, but always came back. And, except for the occasional slice of bread, he still wouldn't take any food, not even the dog food crunchies now bought expressly for him.

When I went around the yard, picking up falling branches for the garbage waste collection, Lonesome followed me at a safe distance. If I happened to go toward him, carrying a branch, his tail went between his legs as he slunk away to his lair behind the azaleas. Gradually, he let me pet his head, but without trust. The feeling was mutual. At my slightest strange move, the dog turned and ran.

I tried to lure him into the garage, wanting to cut off the stringy, matted hair around the neck. Lonesome came for a pat on the head and perhaps a slice of bread; but when he saw the scissors, backed off. I kept trying, speaking softly to him, with an occasional head pat. But the scissors frightened him.

Finally, one day, when I approached, holding the scissors, he gave me a long look and flopped on his side, rolling his eyes toward me. It was as if he said, "Do anything you want with me." I clipped the matted hair and petted him. From then on we trusted each other.

He continued to jog with me. Now he became protective. If another jogger came near me, Lonesome barked at him. He barked at people near our house. Some of the neighbors began to tell us that we should call animal control. We looked at his sad eyes and couldn't do it. By this time Lonesome had accepted my husband as well as me. He never woofed at either of us. Eventually, he barked at the teen-age daughter of a neighbor down the street. She became frightened as he followed her and continued to bark. Her mother called the pound. Joe, my husband, was at work when the truck came.

"Is that your dog?" the animal control man asked me.

"No, he just sleeps here behind the bushes. He doesn't hurt anyone."

"Sorry, I have to take him in. If he's your dog, I'll give you a citation for letting him run loose."

"Wait a minute, please. Let me call my husband."

I went into the house and called. "They went to take Lonesome. Or they will give us a citation. What do you think?"

He didn't have much time to think. "Let them take the dog."

I watched while the man tied Lonesome with a choker knot at the end of the rope. Then he wrapped the end of the rope around the dog's muzzle.

"Why are you doing that?" I asked.

"So he won't bite," the man answered.

"He never bit anyone in his life." It was a guess on my part.

"There's always a first time."

And away he drove with Lonesome looking at me forlornly from a cage in the rear of the truck. My heart was in my shoes.

When Joe came home, I told him what had happened. "I felt bad all afternoon," he said. "Let's go get him."

The next day I called the Orlando Humane Society, describing the dog. They transferred him from the Orange County pound to the shelter. There is a waiting period before anyone can adopt a newly-arrived animal. Frankly, we hoped someone else would adopt him before we did. We had never had a dog.

But, after we visited the shelter a few days later and saw a dejected Lonesome in a small cage, we signed the papers. We paid the forty-dollar fee, which included examination by a veterinarian and neutering. We picked him up and brought him home.

Anticipating this outcome, we had bought a collar and a leash. We couldn't allow him to run loose. We locked him in the garage for the night. He felt trapped and clawed at the door. But when morning came and we opened the door, his fear vanished. He realized that his incarceration had been temporary and accepted the garage as his sleeping quarters every night.

From then on, Lonesome jogged with me. But now, being on a leash, he couldn't challenge anyone else on the street. I did try to experiment unhooking him if I thought no other people were around, but that dog always seemed to find someone. When he put his front paws on a man's shoulders, barking and frightening both the man and me, it was the end of the dog's freedom.

He still didn't eat well. We took him to the animal clinic for the examination that had been part of the adoption contract.

The veterinarian told us that Lonesome had heartworms and hookworms. The latter were easy to get rid of. But the heartworms were a real problem. Because the vet judged our pet to be young—about two years old—he recommended treatment. The treatment is arsenic which, while killing the worms, makes the animal sick. When the drug was administered, Lonesome retched and lost his vigor. One evening, when Joe walked him on our street, the dog collapsed. My husband went home and took the car. Both of us went back to the prone animal. We picked him up bodily, put him in the car, and brought him home.

The vet's gamble that Lonesome would survive the heartworm treatment, paid off. Our pet recovered and became healthy. He joined our menagerie, consisting of six cats at that time, and now, a dog. He weighed fifty-five pounds shortly after his treatment. With good food, he gained ten pounds. We put him on heartworm maintenance and on anti-flea medication.

We discovered that allowing him to run free in our fenced yard was a mistake. He climbed the four-foot chain link fence like a cat. Or burrowed under it like a rabbit. When we hooked him to the fence, he still climbed over. He could have choked. So we attached his leash to a long rope tethered to a corkscrew in the ground. A huge oak protected him from the sun. We left a bucket of water. We didn't think about rain,

One evening, while Joe and I were at a square dance, a thunderstorm struck. "We have to save Lonesome!" We ran from the dance and into the car, reaching home just before the storm hit our house. We put the dog into the garage as the rain began to come down; then went back to the dance. Within a week our yard contained a doghouse. And we could go about our business as usual.

From his location in the yard, he could sniff noses with the cats through the chain link that encloses their "cat corral," challenge the neighbors, and bark at boats passing in the canal behind our house. Or he could curl up in his doghouse. Lonesome also dug a few trenches to keep in practice and curled up in them during the heat of summer days.

Evenings we began to leave him in the house. The cats were assigned to the Florida room. Trusting the dog completely, we could go out if we wished. He began to exhibit the usual canine attributes, like sitting on command, offering a paw, and flopping on his side for petting.

Eventually, people began to tell us that we had a beautiful dog. Visitors shook his paw. Their children hugged him. Relatives wanted to adopt him. And friends were charmed by him. The homeless dog with the sad eyes became a part of the family. He had arrived.

1986

FELINE CHOW TIME

Blackie gets impatient, so he gives the rest a cuff.
Felicia then retaliates; the lady's eight pounds tough.
Sylvie keeps her distance when the other four get rough.

Inky puts his nose down; when it's food, he's in his sphere;
He's a sixteen-pounder and looks bigger every year.
Candy is the timid one, afraid when I come near.

Chow time is a fun time for us owners and our pets,
And though at times their nuisances, we seldom have regrets;
An animal returns in full the kind of love it gets.

1986

ANYBODY WANT A DOG?

In the morning, when I jog him, he decides to scratch and sit,
So I jog in place and wonder when the dog intends to quit.
Or he stops to flop beside me and to have himself a roll;
Then I jog in place and wonder if I'll ever reach my goal.
Next he decorates a tree trunk, and again I have a rest.
I look around and wonder if my neighbors are impressed.
He then wants to relieve himself upon a neighbors' lawn;
I pull him quickly to the road, my patience nearly gone.
He sees a cat and pulls me, and instead of run, I fly.
I huff and puff and wonder if I need this dog, and why.

THE ANSWER

When I sit at night and read a book or watch a TV show,
He puts his head down on my lap, and then I know–I know.

1988

OLD CAT SYLVIE

While cleaning house
I moved her chair-
She looked at where
She always climbed
To reach the table where she slept.

Bewildered, for a moment,
Sylvie stood.
Then tried to climb the table leg
And failed—she turned and saw
The chair at table's other end.

The furry face lit up
With feline awareness.
Then she jumped upon the chair
To reach her table bed.

1989

GONE

He is gone,
My big black beautiful Inky-Cat,
Gone is the sleek and shiny fur
He kept so clean and soft.
Gone is the melodious purr;
Gone, the high-pitched voice
He seldom used.

Gone, the oversize paws
He wrapped around my neck
When picked up, his eyes searching mine.
No longer will he sniff my hair,
No longer sleep upon his back,
Hind legs outspread,
To have his stomach rubbed.

The world goes on and life goes on,
But Inky-Cat is gone.

1989

CANDY

Our next door neighbor in New York took her Dalmation dog to the railroad tracks mornings and evenings. She walked him in the undeveloped area beside the tracks. One day she found an abandoned litter of very young kittens. Two of the animals were dead. The other two were barely alive. She took those home, in spite of the fact that her husband disliked cats.

Someone adopted the little grey tiger cat almost immediately. The other, nearly all white, with calico patches—some forming a question mark on her back—remained. And the kitten existed precariously, considering the dislike of the master of the house.

We had lost two cats. So when our neighbor told us about the plight of the kitten, Joe and I decided to take her. We called her Candy. And, of course, we had her spayed when she reached the right age. Candy was a sweet little thing, timid and fearful. She adapted to our other cats. However, she had a distrust of all things on two legs, a feeling that I could understand.

When we went away for a week or two and another neighbor from across the street took care of the cats, she never saw Candy. The kitten ran out through our pet port and would not return to the house until there were no strange sounds or activities. After we returned, Candy was still suspicious. It took a number of days before she realized that we were her people.

Even so, she didn't completely trust either Joe or me. If I wanted to pick her up, she would run and cry. But if I sat down quietly, she climbed onto my lap and snuggled.

We moved to Orlando in 1978 with eight cats. Tommy was the oldest; then came Betsy, Sylvie, Sooty, Dusty, Curly, Buddy, and Candy. They traveled by air in large pet carriers, two cats in each. We tried to pair them according to personality. We put Candy with Dusty, a bland, sweet-tempered cat. Buddy went with Tommy; Sooty, with Betsy; Sylvie, with Curly. But they all cried before being loaded on the plane. From our position at the airport, we could see the attendants talking to them. Only Sooty—poor, formerly homeless Sooty—seemed to be taking everything in stride.

In Orlando, the rented station wagon held all four carriers as well as us and our luggage. When we arrived in our newly-purchased home, we put the cats in the Florida room. We had the litter box with us. And we had the litter. There was no pet port as yet. The cats could not go out without a human door opener. They had to use the box. We also gave them food and water.

After a week—after they became accustomed to their environment—we let them out at night to explore. And after another week, in the daytime, Then the pet port solved part of the problem. But it needed an enclosure to safeguard them. Before we had the enclosure built, we lost Buddy from feline infectious peritonitis. And, after we built it, because we allowed Sooty out at his loud insistence, someone killed him.

However, this is about Candy. Candy loved the warmth and freedom of our street. There were many hiding places. She ran like the wind. Occasionally, she caught and killed a bird and ate it. Cats cannot buy their birds in the supermarket. Once she killed and ate a duckling.

She was still timid, afraid of Joe, afraid of me. She wouldn't come on call. If she realized we were trying to get her, she would look at us with terror-darkened eyes and increase the distance between herself and us. Her eyes, always wide open in fear or surprise, looked huge in her little pointed face. She weighed only seven pounds—a small cat. She had large ears. The shape of her face and ears was that of a Siamese. She might have had Siamese forebears.

In the mornings she jogged with me, keeping her distance and running ahead of me and far to the side of the road. I tried to stay on her side of the street, as she wanted to be near me. One day I made the mistake of jogging on the opposite side. Candy raced across just as a car came down. She ran into the back wheels of the vehicle. The incident took place behind me, so I don't know exactly what happened. When I heard her cry, I looked back.

She probably had been thrown. I didn't see her. I searched but couldn't find her, If she knew someone looked for her, she would freeze, even if unhurt. All I could do was finish jogging and go home.

That day and the following day and the next, the little cat didn't come to the house. I thought she had been killed. Then she appeared, her white fur grey, the little face looking smaller than usual. She moved slowly, as though in pain. A visit to the vet revealed that she had several broken ribs but no other apparent damage. The vet advised letting her rest quietly. Candy recovered.

Then we had the enclosure built—a chain link cage closed to the roof, accessible by the door from the Florida room and the pet port we added to it. We called it our cat corral.

As always, unusual noises frightened Candy. With strangers in the house, she ran through the pet door and hid under the bushes in the corral. They never saw her, although they knew we had another animal.

She also hid when I vacuumed. The noise of the cleaner terrified Candy. And if Joe was mowing in the corral, or even in the back yard at the same time as the vacuuming, her terror was pitiful. She looked at me with wide dark eyes and tried to hide—somewhere. And meowed, a low-pitched sound; strange, coming from such a small cat. Then I would pick her up if I could and take her into our hall bathroom—or let her go in by herself if she didn't let me lift her. And there she crouched, beside the commode until a half hour or so after the noise from our equipment had ended. We decided to stagger the cleaning and the mowing.

If I tried to return her to the Florida room or the corral, Candy backed away from me. In the bathroom, there was just so far she could back up. I picked her up, petted her and carried her back to her accustomed safety area.

The little feline tried to escape the confinement of house and enclosure. Two or three times, I was careless when I went into the yard, and Candy managed to get out. After her escape, she was first confused, then frightened. She wouldn't come to me or let me get her. A sliding glass door leads from the yard to the Florida room. If I opened it wide enough for a cat to go through, she edged to the doorway, keeping a distrustful eye on me. And back she would go to her haven in the house.

The noise of water from the hose frightened her, as did thunder and lightning, the dishwasher, and the radio. Once, accidentally, we didn't return her to the Florida room after the feeding in the kitchen. And we let Lonesome, our dog, come in for his dinner. The next thing I knew there was a "meow," and saw a seven-pound cat defending herself against a seventy-five pound dog. I rescued her and put her out of harm's way.

When Inky came to live with us, Candy had another cross to bear. The fifteen-pound male thought it great fun to chase Candy and beat her up. He ran after her only when she moved. She tried to stalk carefully across the room when she saw him. But, because she didn't walk normally, Inky still went for her. Then she learned that her best bet was to move only when he slept.

Rascal Inky waited on the Florida room side of the pet port for her to come in. Then it was "get Candy." After I let him have it with the fly swatter a few times—or perhaps after he tired of the sport, he stopped bothering her—after five years of harassment. For the time she had left, Candy enjoyed peace,

I can still see her in the circle chair in the living room, not sleeping, her big eyes wide. In 1984, little Candy left us. The sweet little timid cat was 14 years old when I noticed she wasn't eating. She just pretended. Even when I cooked, especially for her, something that she loved, she didn't give it more than a lick. The vet said she didn't have leukemia. He didn't know what she had. He advised us to get nourishment into her. From the vet we obtained some stuff in a tube. I put some of the goo on her tiny paw. She licked it off and seemed to like it. But there was no real sustenance in the mixture.

She tried eating the other food I gave her. And then the meal started coming up. She stopped eating And one of her front paws gave her trouble. She walked on three legs. Later, even the tube gel, which she liked, came up. It came up as a thick white mucus. I wiped her mouth and tried to feed her again. But it was no use. Her weight went down to four pounds.

I let her into the living room where she would be more comfortable. And she sat on my lap or climbed onto the sofa. Again, I can see her, as I watched her going from me at times, limping into the living room, her skinny little body with its calico question mark on the back, making a beeline for the sofa.

No use, no use. I took her to the vet for euthanasia, but couldn't let him do it. I brought her back home. Another day convinced me I wasn't helping her. So back she went. Her little body is buried in the enclosure as far away from Inky's as possible. He preceded her by two months.

1989

INDIVIDUALS

Animals are fun to watch when left to their own devices. One example is our cat, Blackie. We have an oval braided rug in the kitchen. Blackie pulls himself around the carpet, lying on the floor and propelling himself with his claws. He obviously enjoys this activity the way a child enjoys a merry-go-round. His ears go back, his eyes widen and he increases his speed if there is no obstruction on his route. If one of the other cats is on the rug, either he gives that cat a clout, or the other cat gives him one for the road. If he happens to get close to Felicia, she hisses at him. Felicia doesn't care for fun and games. Sometimes Blackie's enjoyment of his monorail ride is cut short by a wrestling match with Inky who either thinks Blackie's activity is a provocation or has decided, enough of the rug caper is enough.

Lonesome, the dog, is outside. He can come close enough to the cats' enclosure to put his nose against the chain link. He barks at strange cats and chases them, straining to the end of his tether. But he knows our felines. And our cats are his cats. They are not allowed to come into physical contact. Lonesome, being mostly shepherd, is too big and, we think, unpredictable. But from his location, he whines and looks at them from a sphinx position with his tail wagging as a sign of friendship. Blackie accepts Lonesome's gesture and rubs against his side of the chain link barrier. So does our big cat, Inky. But Felicia keeps her distance and Candy is indifferent. Sylvie, knowing that Lonesome cannot reach her, goes up to him on her side of the barrier, with her eyes dark, brow lowered. And she makes her "I don't like you" cat howl. Lonesome is still wagging. If he puts his nose to the chain link, Sylvie spits and strikes like lightning. Lonesome has learned that Sylvie is not to be trifled with.

Inky is curious about our vegetarian meals. At dinner time, this sixteen-pound feline comes to our table and stands on his hind legs with his front paws holding on to the edge. Then he sniffs in all directions to decide if the aroma that comes from our food is worth begging for. It isn't. He goes back to his cat food.

Fred, the duck–and occasionally with a friend or two–sleeps in our back yard. Lonesome is snoozing on the grass or in his dog house. They can come to our sliding glass door or the chain link enclosure and look at the cats. If Lonesome wakens, he lunges at the ducks and there is a flurry of feathers. But Fred flies only far enough to miss Lonesome's range, determined by the length of the dog's rope. And as soon as the dog has settled down again, Fred comes back as though the whole thing never happened. Fred's friends keep their distance.

Blackie is adventurous. He doesn't like being a house cat. He prefers the outdoors, but is not allowed to roam. The sneaky feline follows us, hoping we will open a door, enabling him to dash outside. This has happened a few times. Then he runs right to Lonesome and before the startled dog can react, Blackie has rubbed against him and shown Lonesome that the cat trusts the dog. Once, trying to get Blackie back, I went out and found him under the car in front of the house. The dog, at that time hooked to the garage door, was woofing at him. And Lonesome had a bead of blood on his nose. Blackie might have realized that Lonesome's overtures were not always friendly.

The cats are not allowed in the living room. We have two entrances into that room—one from the hall, one from the kitchen. Blackie races to a door when either Joe or I attempt to open it. We push him back with a foot. Then the door must be closed quickly before Sneaky runs through. Blackie has learned that if we go into the living room from the hall, there is no point in waiting for our return at that spot. He goes to the kitchen door and waits there. We tiptoe back to the hall door and reenter. "Hah, Blackie, fooled you." Sometimes he isn't fooled. He listens to our faint footsteps and goes to the correct entrance. It is a game like, "which cup is over the bean?" The foot is quicker than the ear–sometimes.

Sylvie is frightened by thunder and lightning. When there is a storm, she squeezes herself under a low chest in the Florida room. Neither tidbits nor coaxing can lure her out until the storm ends. Then she emerges, as though the storm never happened.

Candy is afraid of sounds caused by a motor–the vacuum, the lawn mower, the edger, the portable drill or saw, When she hears the vacuum cleaner, she darts from the Florida room through the pet port into the enclosure and hides under the azaleas. If there is mowing also in progress, sometimes she runs back into the Florida room. But the sound of the vac sends her under the bushes again. If I try to reach her, she meows a pitiful, low sound. So I have learned to let her live with her fear until the motor work has ended. Then Candy becomes herself again. Having been an abandoned kitten, she has never lost her distrust of people, even us. We have had her 12 years. She still runs when we make an unusual move or sound and trembles when picked up. However, a pat on the head brings on a purr.

Sylvie is getting old, nearly 14. And she is unsure of herself when trying to reach a chair or high shelf. She discovered that she can climb the back rungs of a chair to reach the seat. Getting down is no problem. Do cats think? Of course!

While, through the years, living with our pets, we have learned to accept their sameness and limitations as a species, their differences as individuals endear them and make animal watching enjoyable.

1990

CONFRONTATION AT THE "C" CORRAL

He was such a gentle cat, the male who suddenly made his appearance on our street. My neighbor who lives two houses down said she fed him. Certainly, he was well-fed. His fur was sleek and his body had the feel of solid flesh beneath the tawny orange coat.

"I can't take him in," my neighbor said. "My cat attacks him. So I feed him outside. I just love him. He's so sweet."

When I petted him, he purred and rolled over. When his paws were lifted skyward, I rubbed his stomach. The purr never stopped.

Joe and I have four cats. Our Sylvie is 15 years old, a mixed-up tortoise shell. She is not very active—just content to sleep, eat a little and drink lots of water. When I pet her, she meows loudly. When I speak to her, she purrs. Sylvie is one of the eight cats we brought with us from New York.

Then we have Blackie. Blackie is a miracle cat. We adopted him from the pound 11 years ago. He has a half-dollar-sized white key on his bib. Otherwise, he is solid black. He is an even-tempered cat who is quick to polish anyone's shoes—or feet, for that matter. Blackie is a talker. Except for the times when he is sleeping, eating, or being petted (when he purrs and polishes), Blackie talks. He is also a sneak, trying to escape from the areas where he is permitted and, when he thinks someone is opening a door, running into the other rooms in the house. He has sneaked outside occasionally, although he is not allowed. But he can't resist sweet talk, and gentle coaxing brings him into the house again. He has managed to get out to our big dog once in a while, to Lonesome's surprise. The cat rubs on the dog and purrs, Before Lonesome can bark and snap, I rescue Blackie.

Then there is Felicia, formerly Felix, given to us by a lady who moved into a no-pet condo. For almost four months Felicia hibernated on top of a cabinet in our family room, coming down surreptitiously when the coast was clear, so that she could eat and drink and relieve herself. I had to struggle with her to make her use the pet port, finally settling on a litter box for those four months. Felicia hissed at the other cats and at us. Eventually, she learned to go through the pet door into our outside enclosure, our "cat corral." Then Felicia calmed down enough to sniff noses with the others, although she gave them a resounding blow if she thought they were too familiar. She also feinted a bite at us and them when she took offense to something we did. However, now at the age of nine, she has become placid. She still won't permit familiarity from the other cats, but she gives them the benefit of the doubt. Felicia is a spooky-colored cat—black with white boots and a white nose and bib. We also have "Kitty Baby," our diminutive name for Jinny, adopted six months ago.

Having these four cats, I should have been satisfied. But there, two houses away, was a sweet gentle orange male who let you rub his stomach and returned the favor by nuzzling against your leg and who looked you in the eyes and meowed softly. Joe and I both loved this cat. I asked my neighbor if I could have him. She was delighted. I went home, brought back the pet carrier and placed the cat inside. With such a trusting animal, I had no problem bringing him home.

I opened the carrier in the cat corral and let him step out. I was prepared for some hostility from our four, but not for what happened. They all raced toward him, ready to attack; screeching, hissing and howling. He hissed and howled also. Then he ran, with the four following. I had to hose them down to stop them. Rusty, as I had named him, climbed the split rail gym we had in the corral and then tried to get out by climbing up the chain link sides. He didn't realize the top was closed, but immediately found out. The warfare ceased for the time being. Joe was at work. I had to go out, although I felt it was unsafe to leave them. When I returned home four hours later, Rusty and Blackie were in the corral on adjoining chairs. I felt I had the situation under control.

Now food time—I emptied the cans, put down the plates. A few cats came in through the pet port. Blackie and Rusty were still in their chairs. I opened the door to let them in. Blackie came, but Rusty remained. His eyes were wild. I picked him up and brought him in for the food. Then it started. First they went after him. Then, when he escaped, they attacked each other. All four cats were hissing, yowling, and striking each other. Fur flew everywhere. I grabbed a broom and started swatting. They ran through the pet port, into the corral.

Sadly, I opened the front door and put Rusty outside. My noble gesture had failed. We couldn't adopt him. Fifteen minutes later, my neighbor called. She had just fed Rusty. A few days later, she called again. Her son, who had an acre around his home in another area, had decided to take the cat.

This story has a happy ending. The gentle cat found a good home. And, in our house, after I had cleaned up all the fur that kept flying around the family room, things returned to normal. The broom-beaten cats forgave me and went back to their usual demonstrations of friendship. They ate the food they had ignored in their vendetta against the newcomer and against each other. I gave Sylvie an extra amount of water in their water bowl.

And, as I write this, they are all snoozing so peacefully that the events following the attempted adoption might never have happened.

1990

JINNY JOINS US

After Inky and Candy died, the house seemed empty. True, we still had three cats and our dog, Lonesome, But Sylvie, Blackie and Felicia were fifteen, eleven and about eight years old, respectively. (We didn't know with Felicia because she was an adult when we adopted her.) These three cats slept a good deal of the time, Also, being depressed at losing big, beautiful Inky and round-eyed sweet little Candy, we needed something to brighten our menagerie and make us laugh again, I wanted an orange cat--it was a long time since we had our Sandy, Ginger, and Nancy in Central Islip. Or, I thought, it would be nice to have a grey tiger or an all-grey feline like our departed Dusty. But I never went out of the way to look for an animal. Somehow, when the situation was right, an adoption resulted.

Almost a month after we lost our two pets, it was right. As I delivered my real estate newsletter two streets from our house, a little orange kitten jumped out from the safety of bushes and began to stalk me. It darted in front of me and behind me. I stooped to lure it close, then petted it. The kitten licked my hand. Did someone own it? I wondered, or was it a stray?

I stopped at a number of houses on that street and asked the occupants if they knew where the kitten belonged. Some had never seen it; others had, but didn't know who owned it. One neighbor gave me a lead. She thought it stayed mostly near one of the houses on the block, then gave me the address. When I went there, I noticed, near the door, a bowl of dry cat food crawling with ants. And two small cats scurried on short legs to the bushes. Neither was the kitten I had come to find.

I left a note at the door of the house. "I would like to adopt a little orange kitten who followed me today. Is it your kitten? Can I have it?" I left my telephone number.

That evening I had a call from the resident. Yes, she was his young cat. A little mother, she had had a litter recently. And her kittens were larger than she. We could have her. He always brought his cats to his plant nursery in Apopka. And people came and took them. He never asked who took them or why. In Florida, the owners of fighting dogs use kittens in the training process. The possible fate of the little cats saddened me. But at least, we could give the mother a good home.

Joe agreed. The next day, with the pet carrier in the car, I drove back to the street and the house. I called, but saw no cats. The bowl of dry cat food was there and a dish with a little water left in it. I went toward the rear of the house. The big screened porch had loads of potted plants in and around it. The screen had been broken. Inside, huddled together and staring at me with suspicious eyes, lay a number of young cats, evidently awakened by my coming. They stood up and began to slink away. Then one cat came forward through the hole in the screen and began to rub against my legs. It was the little mother. What a tiny cat! I picked her up, petting her, put her in the carrier and the car. Home we went.

Inside our house, my first job was acquainting her with her surroundings. She resisted learning to use the pet port; However, after innumerable pushes back and forth by Joe and me, went through. And she turned out to be a terror, She chased the other three cats and spit at them. None could come near her. At five pounds, she even challenged ten-pound Blackie. Except for his tussles with Inky and some early playful attacks on Candy, he was usually calm–a placid old cat.

We named her Jinny. The little thing was five pounds of activity. Everything that moved had sport for her. She went for bugs. She caught the tiny lizards in the enclosure; I rescued them when I could. She was like the wind, a small orange hurricane.

Then she came into heat. She cr-r-r-rowed and cr-r-r-rowed. She stomped the ground with her hind legs and raised her rump for male attention. They came around the enclosure and sprayed to show their maleness. But of course, there could be no contact between the outside cats and ours. Doggie Lonesome acted as a further deterrent to exploring toms. Our yard started to small like a zoo. The three older cats, all neutered, were excited by all the activity. Sometimes they howled in answer to the male threats outside the enclosure.

Inside the house, after the heat routine subsided, she chased the other cats, hissed and became a nuisance. But she also purred and licked my hand when petted. I put catnip on the braided rug in the kitchen. She rolled in the catnip, ate some and fought with the edge of the rug, pulling herself around the entire edge, one paw on top, one underneath.

Joe couldn't stand Jinny's heat activity. "She is in agony," he said. "Have her spayed." I made the appointment, getting her on the county neuter list. Also, an appointment with a fair-priced veterinarian. Whichever could take her first, it would be over a month before she could have the surgery.

In the meantime we had her checked out. She had a slight limp. The X-ray showed a little abnormality in the left hind leg joint. But the vet said to let it alone. Jinny had her shots. A week or two passed. And again Joe said, "Get her spayed. Immediately!"

So I called an expensive vet who took her the next day. He did an excellent job. She was under the weather the first afternoon; then herself again, as if nothing had happened. One of our bedrooms became her recuperating room.

Because of her surgery, we couldn't let her through the pet port into the enclosure. I gave her a litter box and water for the night. And the second day she ate with the other cats in the kitchen.

Jinny calmed down. After about three months, she no longer chased the other cats. She did run after Felicia in sport and tapped the older cat on the back end. Felicia hissed. And Felicia ran. Jinny thought that great fun. We gave her some toys–a catnip ball, a tiny high-bouncing one, wads of paper or foil. But her favorite toys were bugs. By this time lizards had disappeared from the enclosure.

Jinny also played with the two hall runners. They are not fastened to the floor. When she stepped on, we pulled or pushed them with a foot. She pounced on the moving carpet. If we make one butt against the other they rise where they meet. Jinny gripped the ridge. Or she managed to get under the rug. Her eyes widened and her tail swished. Under it we couldn't see her, but we heard her moving, grabbing at the carpet. Another push with my foot and the ridge could be raised or lowered. It could turn into a mound with Jinny under it.

She watched the birds and the squirrels outside the enclosure, with the long intent gaze of the predator. Sometimes she twittered and her tail jerked with her excitement. She crouched and stalked. But the prey was on the other side of the chain link.

The little cat developed a relationship with Lonesome. From the outside of the enclosure he put his nose to the chain link. Blackie had always put his paws through the openings and tried to hit Lonesome's nose. And Lonesome had snapped at him. Now Jinny did the same thing. When Lones first saw her, he knew he looked at a strange cat. He kept looking and barking. However, after I dowsed him with a bucket of water, he realized that he wasn't supposed to attack her vocally, So, after a while, he played with Jinny through the barrier.

Once, after having fed the cats in the kitchen and put them in the Florida room for the evening, and then let Lonesome in for his meal, we heard a strange sound. We ran to see where the noise was coming from, There, preparing to defend herself to the death, spitting, and eyes wide with fear and rage, was five-pound Jinny. Lonesome stood over her, 75 pounds of shepherd/collie/wolf. As we entered the kitchen, he began to bark. We grabbed his collar and pulled him away, then waited for a few minutes until Jinny calmed down. We petted her and put her into the Florida room. Jinny had slipped into the kitchen when I left the sliding door open a few inches. It had been enough for her to squeeze through. And Lonesome had spotted her.

At this writing we still have Jinny. She filled out considerably, now weighing seven pounds. Her coat is a glorious deep orange with barely visible tiger stripes. She still limps a little, but it hasn't slowed her down; still chases lizards when she can find them, and bugs--and monorails the kitchen carpet. She still goes after Felicia and gives her a pat on the rear to hear Felicia hiss. This little "people cat" can be petted in any position, even when she is on her back. She grabs the hand, but meeting no resistance, gives it a lick.

She likes to sleep on the "plank," a board we suspended from the chain link roof of the enclosure. From this vantage point, she can also watch birds and squirrels. Jinny follows me when I scoop the litter area and helps me, hitting the scoop with one small paw, receiving a tap in return, or a bit of sand. Wherever I go in the enclosure, she follows.

In the house she is a bundle of energy. We had forgotten how active a young cat can be. The others sleep. She is around and about and looking for action. And she sits near my chair at dinner time, waiting for a handout. Jinny enjoys a morsel of tofu, vegetable analog, or anything with tomato sauce.

We enjoy watching her, Nothing on television compares with the antics of a kitten at play.

1990

JINNY

Our Jinny is an elf, a sprite,
A blur of orange—a delight;
Who chases feather, leaf and bug;
And monorails the kitchen rug.

She gives our other cats a pat
To make them hiss, provoke a spat;
And patiently sits at my feet
At dinner time, to get a treat.

She streaks from room to room in play
Or stalks imaginary prey.
With playful pluck Jin fights my hand–
She knows I won't misunderstand.

My life changed when I gave myself
A little orange feline elf.

1990

THE YOUNG AND THE AGELESS

I play tag with my little cat, Jinny, in the hall. I chase her. She runs, then stops, crouches and blinks at me. I run from her. She chases me.

I go through the doorway into the kitchen and hide behind the edge of the doorway. She advances cautiously. I peek around it. She looks up at me, then speeds through the doorway past me. I chase her again. She gets into a crouch, ready to spring at my feet.

I push one of the hall runners–there are two–so that they butt against each other and form a ridge where they meet. Jinny hides against the ridge and peers out at me over it, eyes blinking.

Again I push a runner; it forms an arch. Jinny crawls under it and burrows under the carpet. I bounce the little super-active ball, bought for her. She darts out from under the carpet and runs after it. When it stops moving, she attacks the ridge in the carpet. She alternates, hitting the ball, then the carpet, then the ball again.

The play continues until I am worn out. She is still ready to go, tail waving, eyes alert. I think, "What she needs is a kitten to play with." On Jinny goes, looking for excitement. But I have had enough.

Finally she rests on her side with her head up. She looks like a miniature orange lion on a pedestal.

1990

SAY "CHEESE"

My cousin's son, Amir, who was visiting, wanted to take pictures of the three cats and the dog. His camera took such a long time to set up that it was difficult to get them to pose. He started with the cats.

First, he took a picture of Jinny. Jinny was cooperative. She went from the plank where she usually sits, to the "swing" on the fence. And she yawned—a lovely picture if Amir had his camera set. But eventually the shot was taken. So much for Jinny.

Then came Felicia. Felicia was asleep on the loveseat in the Florida room. She awoke, yawned and eyed Amir suspiciously. He focused, refocused, adjusted his gadgets. Felicia sat up, trying to decide whether she was in danger. She decided. She jumped to the floor. Amir followed her, trying to get her attention, refocusing the camera as he went. Felicia darted through the pet port into the cats' enclosure—the cat corral. Amir opened the door and went out after her. Felicia was still suspicious. Amir lifted her to the wooden bench in the enclosure. She jumped down and settled on the plastic chair. He focused for the chair; she jumped down and went under the chair. He focused on her under the chair. She wouldn't turn around and face the camera.

He decided to photograph Sylvie. Sylvie was asleep in the grass. He made noises to get her attention, then focused on her as she awoke and looked at him. By the time he was almost ready, Sylvie decided to investigate the strange object Amir was holding. She walked toward the camera. He walked away from her and around her. She meowed and followed him. I tried to distract her and get her to follow me. She started, then thought it over and decided the camera was more interesting. I picked her up and placed her on the bench. She jumped down immediately and went to Amir. He petted her, lifted her and deposited her on the swing. She jumped down and followed him. I tried to hold her still, figuring any picture, even one including my hands, was better than no picture. She squirmed, turning her head in all directions. Amir kept refocusing the camera. Finally, I managed to get her quiet, with her head up and facing the camera. After I let her go, Amir took the shot.

Back to Felicia. Felicia saw all the activity around Sylvie and decided she herself would be better off in the Florida room. She headed for the pet port. I picked her up and brought her back into the center of the enclosure. Amir refocused the camera. She was intent on getting back into the Florida room and on her bed. However, before she was able to get near the door, Amir took the shot.

Then came the dog, Lonesome. When Amir went into the back yard, Lonesome was glad to see him. Amir petted him and spoke to him. Lonesome's tail wagged, and he flopped. Amir tried to stand him up. Lonesome stood. Then he saw the camera. His tail went between his legs. His ears went down. He wanted to get back to his spot in the corner outside his doghouse and against it. Amir took Lonesome's lead line and pulled him out into the yard where there was sun and light. Lonesome flopped, ears down. His eyes rolled, as he sensed some unknown danger. And he wanted to get out of the hot sun.

I told Amir that Lonesome wanted shade. The man pulled the dog closer to the orange tree. Lonesome lay on the grass and eyed Amir suspiciously, Amir focused the camera. Lonesome didn't know whether to run or stay. Amir spoke to him, gave him a pat and went back to the focusing. Eventually, Lonesome decided that nothing was going to happen to him. His ears went up. Amir did get a shot. I must admit the pose was nice.

I never saw the prints made from the exposures of the fine camera Amir used. But give me my little automatic-focus instant-shot cheapie. The animals have no time to cogitate about the matter. Flash and snap! And I have a picture.

1990

JERRY'S MORNING

I watched Jerry, our young cat, in the Florida room, as he played with the newspaper I had put there for him. Somehow, he arched the center of the sheet so that he could get under it, then scooted around the room with the paper tented over him, making his little cr-r-r-ow sounds and obviously enjoying himself.

Jinny looked on. She probably wondered why Jer was having so much fun, and if she should join the game. For a while he raced around the room under the paper. When he outraced it and was left sans cover, he either returned to the same sheet or found another, whichever happened to be closer. The young male burrowed under the paper, made his tent, and continued to scoot in a circle, "cr-r-r-owing" as he ran. He did this for about a half hour. Bored, Jinny went through the pet port into the outside enclosure.

Eventually, Jerry tired of that game. But he wasn't finished with the newspaper. His hunter instinct asserted itself. He clawed at a sheet, bunched it up, and began to tear at it as if it were prey. No time for "cr-r-row, cr-r-r-ow." The paper gave him no resistance, and he derived no satisfaction from shredding it. After making a mess for a minute or so he went under the table in the kitchen and lay down. But only for a few seconds.

He came to me as I sat at the table writing this, stood up on his hind legs with his front paws on my knee and purred as I petted him. That took no more than a minute. Then he was off to find new diversions–but kept coming to me, lifting his paws to my knees. Finally, he jumped on my lap. I continued to write. The corner of the pad overlapped the edge of the table.

Jerry became interested in that, both with an exploratory paw and his mouth. I blocked him.

Puss still wanted excitement. He took care of a few itchy spots as he lay on my lap. But, in between licking and checking, his gaze traveled to the ceiling, to the view outside the sliding glass doors, to old cat Felicia who paced between the kitchen and the Florida room.

I became tired of writing and holding the good-sized cat on the lap. I carried him to the Florida room and placed him on his favorite sleepy spot. He immediately jumped down, went to the bowl of dry cat food, and began to replenish his energy.

A half hour later, I had almost completed this little sketch. Jerry had finished his snack and now lay on his perch, sleeping. There, with an occasional lick of a paw, he would remain for the rest of the day. That was Jerry's morning.

1990

CHOW TIME

When I fed the cats in the kitchen, Felicia usually ate from the dish farthest from the Florida room and near the kitchen cabinets. Knowing that the first cats entering the kitchen go to the nearest plate, I put down only two, figuring that Jerry would rush in and go to the closest meal, while Felicia would pass him to eat in her accustomed spot. Instead, one day, Felicia came in ahead of him and went to the first dish, while Jerry went past her to the place where she usually ate.

Next I set a plate down still closer for Jinny. And nearest to me, one for Sylvie who always needed coaxing to come into the house from our enclosure. They both came into the kitchen and started eating. All was well until Felicia realized that Jerry was eating from "her" dish. She stood by him and invited a confrontation. Jerry kept eating. Finally, Felicia gave up and went back to the food she had abandoned.

By this time Jinny and Sylvie had finished for the time being and left the kitchen. So Jerry had a choice. He decided to sample what remained of their dinners. Felicia went to her usual spot, which was now available, and continued to eat. Soon all the other cats, including Jerry, left. Felicia alone ate while three locations remained sans cats. And she ate from "her" dish.

After she indicated that she had finished, I returned all the cats to the Florida room, closing them in. Then I consolidated their leftovers into two plates and took those into the room so that the cats could clean them during the evening.

I had one in my left hand, one in my right. I placed the left one down first. Felicia ran toward it and began to eat.

Jerry ran for that one also. I put the right hand dish behind Felicia a moment later. Jerry didn't even turn around. Instead, he pushed Felicia's head out of the first one and commenced to clean up the contents while she stood staring at him, trying to figure out what had happened. But the little female didn't look behind her. Instead, she kept watching Jerry as he ate. I guess she thought that he would leave her something.

Then Joe and I took our dog, Lonesome, out for his run, When we returned, both the cat dishes were cleaned out. Either he or she—or any of them—had discovered the other plate. I went into their area and picked up the dishes for washing. Now they could go back to their crunchies, which were always available.

1990

LONESOME AND THE VISITOR

The doorbell rings. Lonesome, our dog, who has just had his meal and is in the house for the evening and night, barks wildly. We pull him away from the door and lock him in the kitchen until we see who is outside, and if our visitor likes dogs--big dogs. From the kitchen, Lonesome continues to bark.

It turns out to be a neighbor on personal business. And she isn't afraid of large canines. So we can let Lones back into the living room. We open the door from the kitchen. He bounces out as though shot from a gun and right to the lady, dancing around her, still barking.

"His name is Lonesome."

"Good dog," she says, "Good Lonesome, give me your paw."

She pats his head. He calms down, then licks her hand.

She takes a seat. He follows her. She pats his head again, and his back. "Good boy," she says, "good dog." Lonesome's eyes roll. Then, without any preliminaries he holds up a paw.

"Shake," she says, "atta boy, good Lonesome."

For a few moments they hold their pose, the dog's paw in her hand.

Suddenly Lonesome flops at her feet, eyes again rolling, looking at her sideways. He is comical, tongue out, trying to focus on her face. She rubs his stomach. The hind leg that is on top goes in the air. Except for that and those eyes, he plays dead.

For a few minutes she rubs his stomach and his back. His hind leg remains in the air, twitching occasionally. Then she stops to state her business and make conversation. Lonesome remains in his prone position at her feet for another minute or so. Suddenly realizing that he is not getting any attention, he sits up and barks. She pats his head, and one front paw goes into a "shake" position.

"Good dog."

"Bye, I must go. Bye, Lonesome."

He sees her get up and head toward the door. Our pet's moment of glory is over. He will be ignored again like a piece of furniture. He protests, barking furiously. We hold him as we open the door for our departing neighbor.

Lonesome continues to bark for a while. Perhaps he is hoping she will come back. Then he quiets down and becomes our uncomplaining house dog. He finds his favorite spot on the carpet, lies down and snoozes.

1990

BLACKIE

Joe's father stayed with us during two winter seasons. His favorite cat was Blackie, whom we adopted from the pound. This little feline, all black except for a white spot on his chest–the spot is called a "key"– was a talker. Pa loved him and permitted him into the guest room and on the bed.

After his special friend left for the summer in New York, Blackie ran into the hall each day and positioned himself in front of the guest room door, meowing continuously. His wail sounded like "Meh, meh, meh, meh." He did this for the entire time Joe's father wasn't with us, even for the four or five years that Pa didn't come at all. A number of times he managed to sneak into the now-deserted room.

A shoe polisher, he would flop when petted and rub his head on our feet. He would roll and roll as long as he was petted or acknowledged. He could be touched in any position, even when on his back. Blackie was a peaceful, sweet-tempered feline. The only times he growled were when the veterinarian took his temperature with the rectal thermometer or when his bouts with Inky became too violent.

He was lively–the first to come into the kitchen when he heard the can opener. And he was a jumper and a climber. His big eyes were always partly closed–half moon eyes.

One of the endearing things he did was perch on the two adjacent arms of the plastic chairs that stood side by side in the enclosure. From that location, he would survey the activity in the area. Or, more often, he would snooze, with his head hanging down, I tried to photograph him in this position, but as soon as he heard me come out into the corral, his head went up. Through the kitchen window, I made a rough sketch of him.

A number of times, always trying to escape, he managed to get out of the house and into the yard. After a few moments of rejoicing in his freedom–climbing trees, running like the wind, snooping in the neighbor's yard–he would come on call. I petted him and brought him in, a prisoner again.

When I think of him, I remember his big eyes, his chubbiness (he weighed 10 pounds), his shiny black coat with that half dollar key on his chest, his especially fat tail, his "meh, meh, meh," his rolling at the feet, his sweet disposition.

Blackie died of leukemia. He was probably 12 or 13 years old. We buried his body next to that of his friend Inky in the cat corral.

1991

CAT JERRY

Some carpeting is Jerry's toy-
A small square three by five.
He exudes happiness and joy;
How great to be alive!

He leaps on it with all four paws,
Or hits it like a ball;
He grabs at it with outstretched claws
And shoves it to the wall.

He burrows under, makes a tent,
And races round the room.
With carpet cover, he's content
To scurry, dart and zoom.

He talks to it with chirps and mews-
I laugh to see him play;
My work is waiting, but I choose
To watch him every day.

1991

FUN AND GAMES

The cats are in the cat enclosure--the "cat corral." Jerry, less than a year old, sits on the plank, the highest spot over the split-rail fence. Jinny, about 18 months old, climbs to the top rail, right under Jerry. She bats at his tail, then gives his tail a nip. He swings down at her. He has the advantage because he is higher. Jinny is getting the worst of it. She climbs onto the plank, gives Jerry a nip and then springs down to the lower rail and to the ground.

She hides under the heather bush. He leaps over the bush and jumps her, There is a short tussle. She runs to the fence and onto the "swing" that is attached to the fence; then rushes at him. Both cats spring high in the air. They wrestle. A moment later, both scoot through the pet port into the Florida room.

Once in the Florida room they forget what they had been doing. Jerry takes the high road over the end tables and chairs. Almost immediately both cats go out through the pet port into the enclosure. They chase each other again. After a short run, Jinny leaps onto one swing, Jerry onto the other.

A moment of quiet. Jinny jumps from the swing and races toward the pet port. She stops to consider whether to pass through or remain outside. In the meantime, Jerry has also jumped from the swing. Jinny turns to run at him. Both spring high in the air and collide. She returns to the swing. He runs into the Florida room through the pet port.

There he lies down next to the sliding glass doors and watches the squirrels for a second, then advances to the dry food cat bowl. He scoops a few crunchies out of the bowl and, when they fall to the floor, eats them.

Jinny bursts into the Florida room. And immediately out. She climbs back up the split rail fence and onto the plank, where she dozes. Jerry runs back out to look for diversions. He doesn't see anything to interest him, He returns to the Florida room, goes to his favorite chair and falls asleep.

During all this time, the other two cats--sixteen-year-old Sylvie and ten-year-old Felicia, have been sleeping.

1991

JAMIE

The first time I saw the pale orange female cat was in front of the house next to mine. She half-crouched, sniffing the sidewalk. She had the look that a cat gets when it is not cleaning itself; when it is either sick or hungry.

I went into my house, picked up a box of cat crunchies and went back next door. I put a handful of food on the walk. The cat began to eat voraciously. As she ate, she snuffled, a strange sound I had never heard before. Obviously she had gone hungry for some time. I petted her. She was not fat, but not bony either. She wasn't afraid of me. Someone must have taken care of her not too long ago. But who and where?

A call to all the neighbors who were animal friends proved fruitless. Some had seen the cat, but no one knew where she had come from. She didn't belong to anyone on our street. "Same old story," I thought, "abandoned." Now and then someone leaves an unwanted animal in our community. Sometimes it finds a home. That was how we acquired our dog Lonesome and our cat Inky.

The cat disappeared for a few days. Then I saw her again. She was obviously pregnant, explaining the abandonment. Someone had been too ignorant, too cheap, or too uncaring to have her spayed. And too irresponsible to bring her to the humane shelter. When she became pregnant, they brought her to our area and dumped her to fend for herself.

I left word with all my neighbors to watch her. When she had the litter, I would take her to the humane society. I put some food in front of my neighbor's house, but the squirrels ate it. Some people down the street reported seeing her. But for a week, I had no sight of her.

On a Sunday, the lady who lives on the cul-de-sac at the far end of our block, knocked on my door.

"Your cat had kittens in my garage," she accused. "Come get them."

"The cat isn't mine," I told her. "But if you keep her and the kittens until Tuesday, I will take her and them to the humane shelter. Let me see where she had the litter. Wait a minute. I'll get some cat food."

I followed her. In her garage, under a tool bench, tucked as far back as she could get, lay the little mother. She nursed five kittens. I put the crunchies on the floor. The cat didn't come out.

"Let's go away and let her eat. She's probably afraid of us."

We left. I assured the lady that, since the humane shelter was closed on Monday, I would take the cats the following day.

That evening I prepared a laundry basket for the kittens. And I had our cat carrier for the mother. And Tuesday morning I went to get the cats. The kittens were easy to pull out gently with a rake. But the mother was frightened. She crouched as far back in the corner as possible, away from us.

The homeowner suggested drastic measures.

"Wait, let me try again. Please move back." I put my hand toward the cat, my fingers curled as though I had something in my hand. She came forward slowly, curious. My neighbor breathed a sigh of relief. And we were on our way.

The humane society clerk told me that the shelter didn't hold nursing mothers and new litters. They were unadoptable and were put down immediately. But if someone could keep them for five weeks, the kittens and mother could be put up for adoption. She looked at the tiny ones. One of them was pure white. "I know I could find a home for that one," she said.

I couldn't take them. I had four cats, two of whom would kill the newborns. From the shelter desk I called the owner of the garage where the litter had been born.

"Would you keep the cat and kittens just five weeks?" I asked. "I would bring food. Then they would have a chance to be adopted."

She responded immediately and clearly. "Absolutely not."

I looked at the clerk. "I would keep the mother, but I can't take the litter. Isn't there some way they can be saved?"

"It doesn't hurt them, and it's quick," she soothed. "We just give them an injection."

"I guess that's it." She gave me a paper to sign. Tears, without my control, were gushing down my face. Subconsciously, I reacted as I had when our little cat Candy had to be euthanized.

Gently, the clerk removed the kittens from the laundry basket. I picked up the basket and the carrier with the mother cat and took them back to the car. During the drive home, the little cat cried a few times.

"You'll have a good home," I told her. I wondered whether the four cats at home would accept her and how she would respond to them. I knew Joe would like her.

At home, I fed and petted her–she rubbed and purred–and took her into the enclosure, our "cat corral." She ran on short legs to the far end of the enclosure, went behind the hibiscus bush, which gave her some protection, and crouched there unhappily. Moments later, Jerry and Jinny came running through the pet port and into the enclosure. They both tried to get at the newcomer, but she had chosen her spot well. There was a lot of hissing, nothing else.

Every feeding time I brought her into the house and watched her to make sure the others didn't bother her while she ate. Old cats Sylvie and Felicia weren't aggressive, but Jinny and Jerry felt they had to get rid of the intruder.

Joe and I took her to the vet for shots and a checkup and made the appointment for spaying. That would be two months later. The vet said that she was a young cat.

Little by little she gained confidence and came out from behind the hibiscus. But she still favored the far end of the enclosure where the chain link protected her against attacks from the rear.

We named her "Jamie"–another J. She purred and stomped when petted. But she ran from us when we approached her. Then she had to be coaxed back. Slowly her milk dried up and her stretched stomach returned to normal size.

To the vet she went for spaying.

"What a beautiful cat," someone said.

"Thank you. She was dumped."

And then she was spayed and home again. She had to be kept inside for a while with a litter box, but she desperately wanted to go out into the enclosure. We kept her in sick bay for four days. Then we let her out. She learned the pet port immediately. This, in spite of the fact that rascal Jerry stood by to swat her as she came in or went out.

The spaying was well-done. Soon, with plentiful food and a good home, her self-image improved. She began to sleep closer to the pet port but still outside. She came in at will and ate some of the crunchies which are always available in the Florida room. When Jerry or Jinny challenged her, her ears went back and she put up a defensive paw. They both backed off.

Although still timid, Jamie made friends. She rubbed and purred and stomped. She became fastidious. She cleaned her gold-bronze fur until it shone. She ate and she ate. Her period of starvation gave her a feline philosophy. "Food is good." She became pettable, then chubby. And suddenly, Jamie began to play.

She didn't go after lizards the way the bad boy Jerry did. Although she watched him a few times, that play didn't turn her on. Her toy was a bit of a leaf or a twig. Joyfully, she would leap into the air and pounce on the leaf. And run circles around it. And do a little cat dance. The fur on her back ridged down the center of her spine as she danced. She obviously had good health and high spirits.

The final stage in Jamie's development became interaction with the other young cats, Jerry and Jinny. By this time, our old cat Sylvie had become terminally ill and had to be put down. And old Felicia remained her usual grouchy self, hissing and growling at any cat who came within a foot of her. But the other two cats began to include Jamie in their games.

Now they play tag in the enclosure, climbing up the gym Joe made for them. When one goes through the pet port, another runs after, giving the departing tail a swat with a soft paw. Jamie waits for one of the other cats to come in, and a little confrontation ensues.

Jerry's idea of playing is to approach Jamie and try to give her a shot. But Jamie is equal to the occasion. She trades pat-a-cake for pat-a-cake. It is all good-natured. No nails are out, and no one growls or hisses.

Jamie follows me when I go into the kitchen or hall. But wen I turn around she runs like the wind. It is funny to see such a chunky cat move so fast. She knows I won't hurt her. She is playing her brand of tag.

She looks into our eyes now, her green eyes calm and beautiful in their golden surroundings. My only regret is that her litter was lost. But there is always an overabundance of animals at the shelter. Some must die that others might find a home. At least Jamie was a lucky one.

1992

UNIQUE
(Johnny)

A stray kitten, barely returned to life
After near-death by starvation,
Becomes an individual-
Demanding love, demanding food,
Demanding attention-
Meowing, purring, rubbing
On his benefactor.

"Look at me," he says, "I am me;
I am real, I am a soul,
Unique, in my tiny body."

His eyes are bright and deep.

1992

WOOGA-WOOGA

I called the female dog, "Wooga-wooga." That was the way I translated her barking when she first chased our car in the 33rd Street Industrial Park. We take Lonesome, our dog, there every morning and evening for what used to be a short run and is now a walk, as the aged canine plods instead of prances. There, at 6:30 A.M. and 6:30 P.M., with few people at their places of work, he can roam freely without a leash. And he can relieve himself. Joe carries a small coal scoop in the car and picks up if the dog honors a concrete surface. On grassy areas, since we do not use the same parking lot every day, insects, bacteria and other natural forces break down the droppings and provide fertilizer for the greenery.

Wooga-wooga, a mixed breed brownish dog weighing perhaps 50 pounds, discovered Lonesome on one of our walks. After a few rather unfriendly overtures, she kept her distance—probably because she realized that he outweighed her by over 25 pounds—and went back to her home turf, the Chiquita Banana property, there squatting to demarcate her territory. When we put Lonesome back into the car and took off, the dog chased the car, barking as she ran. We marveled at her speed. She did 25 miles an hour. Her "wooga-woogas" complemented Lonesome's high whine. Joe got a kick out of this duet. We both felt glad that she enjoyed the chase, and our dog seemed to be enjoying her activity.

One day she miscalculated and ran into our moving car. She howled, picked herself up and ran off. We stopped the car. I went to the door of the banana company office, opened it and entered. The receptionist looked at me.

"We hit your dog. She ran into our car."

" Cindy ?"

"We don't know where she is now. We hope she will be all right."

"I'll go look for her."

She went out, and we went back to our car and drove home.

The next day we didn't see Wooga-wooga, now known to us as Cindy. We worried about the little dog. But the day following, and every day after that, except for an occasional Sunday when the employees probably locked her behind the fence that surrounded the Chiquita parking lot, she chased—and chases—our car.

One day, with Cindy hot on our tail, another car that had been following at a safe distance, pulled up beside us as the barking dog dropped behind to claim her territory with a squat and a wet. The driver of the other car beeped us. Joe slowed down and she opened the window.

"Did you lose a dog?" the lady asked. "She was right behind you. Did you forget her?"

We laughed and explained what had happened. And she laughed too. We went our separate ways.

It is over eight years since Cindy started chasing our car. Lonesome must be close to 12 years old. And Cindy must be at least eight. If we let him out on a parking lot near her domain, she wooga-woogas at him and follows him, but at a safe distance—always indicating by a squat and a wet, that he is trespassing. If we approach her, this Chiquita watch dog turns and runs, tail between her legs. Her bravery ends with the car.

No matter where in the industrial park we take Lonesome, Joe always drives by the Chiquita property on our way back, giving Cindy a chance to chase the car. Lonesome whines and the chunky little female wooga-woogas and runs like a greyhound. Joe and I both get a great deal of pleasure out of this activity.

1992

HE-ERE'S JOHNNY!

My neighbor Lenore, stood on her covered patio, tending to some potted plants. Her two dogs and cat were in the house.

From the corner of her eye, she saw a slight movement in the bushes at the edge of the yard.

Lenore watched the spot where she had seen the movement. Again, an almost imperceptible something caught her eye. She approached cautiously. If it were a snake or a wild animal, she stood a good chance of being bitten. When she came close enough, she saw what might have been a kitten. It was a tiny skeleton covered with tan skin. From the head a pair of frightened amber eyes looked out.

She put out a finger in friendship. A faint meow followed by a louder purr came from the little thing. Encouraged by its apparent friendliness, she picked up the tiny animal and brought it to the patio. The whole time she carried it, the sounds alternated between meowing and purring. And the head began to rub on her hand. On the patio, she tried to stand it on the table she used for tending houseplants. It fell.

"I thought its legs didn't work," she told me later, "but I had to get it to eat something." She went into her kitchen, filled a small dish with some canned kitten food from her cat's larder, and a pan with water, returning with them to be greeted by a meow and a purr. The kitten hadn't stirred from where she had put it. The food in front of it didn't seem to tempt it. The animal wouldn't or couldn't eat.

Lenore first called her daughter who is an animal lover, and then me. Debbie brought a fiberglass animal carrier the size for a medium large dog, She checked out the kitten and tried to put food into its mouth. The kitten didn't eat, but rubbed and purred, seeming to appreciate that it was being treated kindly. Debbie put the little animal into the carrier.

I came because I had indicated to Lenore that we might be interested in adopting another cat. At that time we had Felicia, Jinny, and Jerry. But this little one, on the brink of starvation, would be no match for the three well-fed, mature felines. I ran my finger along the kitten's spine. Just bones. Except for the rib cage and the head, it was completely nothing.

"Perhaps it's too young to eat solid food. Do you have milk?" My neighbor did. She poured some into a small dish and put it before the kitten. It looked but didn't make a move to drink.

"OK, kitten," I said, "you have to eat something." I put my finger into the milk and dabbed some on its chin. That didn't do anything; perhaps not enough. I pulled the kitten's head down gently and dipped its chin into the milk. Some went into the mouth. Suddenly the little thing started lapping. I had primed the pump. It didn't finish the milk, but turned from that dish toward the kitten food–and began to eat!

"I couldn't take this kitten. Our cats would kill it. Maybe you could keep it a little while and then take it to the humane society. If it ate a little and put some flesh between the skin and bones, it would be adoptable. It's a semi-long-hair. And with those pretty eyes and that friendly purr and rub, and all that talking, it would find a home, I'm sure."

She looked at me as though I had told her to kill the kitten. "I'll feed it for a while, and then see. But something is wrong with the hind legs. It can't stand up."

I picked up the small bundle of skin and bones–the baby weighed less than a pound–and tried to stand it up. The little thing stood unsteadily and then lay down.

"I don't think anything is wrong with the legs. It's just weak."

That was on a Monday. The humane shelter was closed.

"You can bring it tomorrow,"

"I'll keep it until Thursday; then I'll see."

I had reports of the little animal's progress–eating, and the legs were all right. It stood up by itself now. Did we want it? Did I want to see it?"

I went to her house and looked at the kitten again. It lay in the carrier on the table. It welcomed me with a meow and purr and rubbed its head against my finger when I went to pet it. Little bony animal!

The next day Lenore phoned. "Let me know if you want it," she urged. "But if you take it and change your mind, don't take it to the humane society. I'll think of something else.'

"Joe, do we need a kitten? Do you want to look at it? We'll have to keep it away from the other cats until it gets a little bigger. What do you think?"

"I'll go look." He went to the patio two houses down. The baby cat went through its meowing, purring, rubbing routine. Joe examined it. "He's a little male. I guess we can take him." I think those big amber eyes did it. Our three cats have green eyes. And Joe liked the little fellow's personality and semi-long-haired blonde coat.

On Saturday, I picked up the tiny cat, now chipper. He stood without tottering. His mentor had treated him for fleas. She gave me the can of flea powder and the cans of food. And told me again, "Remember, if you don't want the kitten, don't give him to the humane society."

As I write, it is Thursday. The baby cat is eating almost continuously. He uses the litter box, covering up with athletic zeal. He doesn't like milk or water, but eats adult cat food as well as the donated kitten food. He now weighs nearly two pounds. Almost imperceptibly, the vertebrae are less sharp. He is isolated in our Florida room, that part which is not available to the other animals. He meows and purrs when we are near and follows us all around the room. He even climbs a little. However, there does seem to be something wrong with one hind leg. He has adopted the crocheted cat napper I put down for him And who knows–with his fierce hold on life, he may turn out to be a beauty. His name–for such a talker–Johnny, what else. He-ere's Johnny!

* * *

An addition to this history. Johnny was allowed to eat with the other cats after a week of isolation. They accepted him, evidently not feeling threatened by his meow and purr. Although the veterinarian couldn't help the bad leg, Johnny ran almost normally. He learned to use the pet port and zoomed in and out. He grew to ten pounds with a glorious blonde long-haired coat. And he continued to make his presence known by his talking. That's Johnny!

1993

RUSTY AND LONESOME

Rusty is a cat, so named because his fur is a deep orange. Lonesome is a shepherd-type dog who, as an abandoned canine, was given his name inadvertently, He was a friendless dog, a lonesome dog; the name remained, even after he adopted us.

A mother cat, six homeless kittens, and two adult males looked for food from dusk to dawn daily, Some people fed them. I fed them. They were wild. It was obvious that what we had was a cat factory, And that it was necessary to be cruel to be kind. The cats had to go.

After filling out the appropriate complaint form, and after numerous calls, one to a county commissioner, we obtained from Orange County Animal Services a humane trap. Somehow, I couldn't bring myself to use it, although I realized it was necessary. My next-door neighbor took the trap and set it.

In the meantime, two kittens disappeared. Then my neighbor trapped one male and took it to Animal Services. And, one at a time, he trapped three kittens. I had taken a fancy to a little blue-eyed white male with extra toes on his front paws. We took him from the trap and adopted him, naming him Mitty for his mitten-toes. Then the last kitten was trapped. One adult male and the mother cat remained, The female went to a neighbor two houses down the street. But the male remained near our house. I put food out for him. Actually, I hoped he would be trapped too. But this cat happened to be shrewd or lucky. Animal Services recalled the trap, and he was safe for the time being.

He ate the food I put out for him in the evening. Sometimes he asked for food in the morning, but he usually shared breakfast with the mother cat down the street. During the day he disappeared. Eventually, we discovered his hiding place; he nestled in the crotch of our live oak tree, more than 20 feet above the ground. Lonesome, whom we tethered at the garage entrance mornings and evenings, barked furiously at the cat.

Then, one evening, when we opened the door for Lonesome, the cat came out of the garage. Somehow he had, at the risk of being attacked by the dog, managed to get past the canine during the morning. From that time on, the cat slept indoors. He waited his chance. When Lones was sleeping or inattentive, he stealthily made his way past the big dog and jumped to the top of our garage wall storage cabinets, where he had found a safe place to spend the day. I put a litter box down for him.

Orlando summers are hot. Although, when home, I opened the doors to create a breeze for the animal, most of the time the cat endured our 100 degree temperature during the day.

Little by little, Lonesome stopped snapping at the feline, and now and then the cat would go up to the dog and rub on the astonished canine. When Lonesome had enough of this show of affection he would woof at the cat, who would hiss and distance himself from Lones. By this time we had accepted full responsibility for feeding this feline. We began to call him Rusty, and he was our pet. After Lonesome started to tolerate him, Rusty had no difficulty entering the garage, It became his apartment, his home, Eventually, the dog and cat developed a sort-of friendship. Lonesome no longer woofed; Rusty could rub against him and even lie down next to him with complete trust.

People, he didn't trust. Although we could give him an occasional pet, most of the time he jumped at our touch as though he had an electric shock. Then the mother cat down the street had another litter. I took some of the kittens to animal control. It was obvious that Rusty, who might have been the father, could not be allowed to continue mating. He had to be neutered.

Our vet has a waiting list. We made the appointment. Rusty would be taken two months from that date, The vet agreed to give us a tranquilizer for Rusty. We would put it into the food, so that we could lift him into the pet carrier.

One day I coaxed Rusty into the house. And, like a previous attempt to bring in an adult male cat, this action brought on a battle royal. Our indoor cats attacked the newcomer. At that time we had Jinny, Jerry, Jamie, Johnny and Mitty. I managed to lock them in the Florida room. But I didn't know how to get Rusty out of the hall where he had ensconced himself to fend off his attackers. He had the advantage of walls on three sides.

He remained in the hall all night, producing an effluent with a horrible stench and wetting our hall runner with his male musky urine. But, in the morning, he had had enough of the hall and the house. When I opened the front door, he edged himself out. I cleaned the runner as best I could, removing the stool. Then I took the carpet outside, sponged it with soapy water and hosed it down. When it dried, I sprayed it with Urine Kleen, a pet product.

In the two months before he was neutered, Rusty fathered another five kittens. The neighbor, two houses down, assumed the task of feeding them. Of course, they were wild. And if not neutered or trapped, would mate with each other and multiply. However, Rusty (now our cat) was our immediate concern.

Neutering time came for him. With the tranquilizer, it was easy to put him into the cat carrier and take him to the vet. We picked our puss up the following day. He recovered from the surgery almost immediately. With regular feeding, he developed into a beautiful animal. His deep orange fur became lustrous; he filled out; his amber eyes were bright and clear.

Rusty never came into the house again. He loved the garage, his home. As the winter came on, we gave him a heater and a crocheted "cat napper." He made friends with some of the outside wild cats and kittens. And he roamed with them a few hours at dawn or in the evening. However, his special friend was–and is–Lonesome.

When Lonesome is in the garage, before or after our semi-daily car trips to the industrial park where he can run free and relieve himself, Rusty rubs against him and nuzzles him. Lonesome sniffs at the cat, but he doesn't woof or act antagonistic. And if it is cool, Rusty snuggles up to his big friend, and the two enjoy mutual warmth and companionship.

When we go away for a few days, Rusty gets locked out of the garage, and our next-door neighbor gives him food and water, Lonesome spends these days in a kennel. Rusty probably goes back to the haven near the top of our live oak tree. And on our return, he resumes his life where he left off–with his garage apartment and his canine friend.

1993

CAT CIRCUS

In an effort to slow down the burgeoning feral cat population, my neighbor, Lenore, and I decided to have them all neutered. There was a regularly-pregnant female cat, five nearly adult kittens—one of which was a female—and, just as we decided to defuse the population bomb, a new litter.

I consulted with a veterinarian in a close-by elite subdivision. He understood our objectives and said that he could take a cat immediately, with no appointment. Our usual vet has a two-month waiting period. This vet also said he would negotiate the fee. That sounded good. My next move was to contact the Orlando Humane Society (OHS). The people there sympathized with our effort and promised us a trap.

Lenore was feeding the cats. When I picked up the trap at OHS I gave it to her, with instructions for setting it. The next morning she called. A cat had been trapped. It was one of the male teen-age kittens. I brought him to the facility where the veterinarian would perform the surgery. The next morning, as I was unavailable, Lenore's daughter drove her to the animal hospital and picked up the cat. They also picked up a bill for $45, which they paid. Our usual vet charges $25 for this surgery, with $13 additional for the shots. So this man's fee—he threw in the shots—was out of line. I reimbursed Lenore half. But there were just too many cats. Our objectives were unreal. We would have to let the humane society take them. Lenore didn't like that. She loved those cats. So, after that, she didn't set the trap.

Then I decided to do something about the problem. I started to feed the older kittens in the garage when I fed our cat Rusty. There were four animals—two males, the neutered male whom I didn't want, and a little female, obviously pregnant. I contacted OHS again. Dean, they said, would pick up the female if I could keep her in the garage. They would abort the litter and spay the mother. No charge. And I made an appointment with our inexpensive vet to neuter one of the males.

By this time I had named them so that when we talked about them we knew which was which. Our cat, the deepest orange, we had called Rusty. The darkest of the kittens, a lighter orange, I named Sandy. The female, a pale tan, would be Blondie. The other male, for obvious reasons, was Whitey. I ran out of colors for the neutered male. So, since he was closest in color to Sandy, I dubbed him Randy. I targeted Sandy to go to the vet. But either he or Whitey would go, depending on which I could catch.

On the Monday before the Tuesday scheduled for OHS investigator, Dean, to pick up Blondie, Joe noticed a leak near our hot water heater in the garage. Not only did the water ooze out there, but the carpet inside the house was getting wet. Joe turned off the water in front of the break in the pipe and called the local handyman. Charlie heard the desperation in Joe's voice. He would come the next day.

Tuesday, the day we expected Dean, Charlie arrived to locate the leak and make the repair. The leak seemed to be in the wall of the house between the garage and the living room. Since I had a scheduled meeting that morning, I cautioned Joe, "Don't open the garage door. Don't let the cats out until Dean comes." "O.K.," said my husband.

After the meeting, when I came home, a wide-open garage door greeted me. Charlie had brought in a compressor, had blasted through the concrete in the floor of the garage and the wall of the house, He had exposed the corroded pipe, removed and replaced it with plastic. I called OHS and explained our predicament. Obviously, Blondie would not go to the vet that day. All the cats were outside, in hiding.

Wednesday, the cats were still leery of our house. Charlie came back and filled in the holes he had made in floor and wall. It was late afternoon when he finished. No OHS Wednesday.

Thursday, although the cats were still ill-at-ease in the garage, I managed to feed them there. Blondie, Rusty, and Randy came. Sandy and Whitey were nowhere to be seen. Later, however, a little before noon, both appeared. One garage door had been closed the whole time. I was able to close the second door, then called OHS.

"Is the cat in the garage?

"Yes, she is."

"Dean will come as soon as he can."

At about 5:00 Dean called to say he couldn't make it, "I've been on the run all day, and it's late. I've just returned to the shelter," And Blondie began to give birth.

On Friday, when I called again, Dean came in late afternoon. He had a cage and a long pole with a snare at one end. By this time, Blondie had produced three kittens in a shallow cardboard box—really a tray—near the garage door. I cautioned Dean not to say anything. I thought his voice might frighten her. However, after a few minutes, he came back into the house.

"She ran. I didn't want to hurt her, She is very frightened. But I put the tray with the kittens in the cage and left the cage door open. Maybe she'll come back to them. If she does, shut the door. I have to leave."

"Tomorrow is Saturday. Is OHS open?"

"Yes, we open at 10:00." Dean left.

Blondie did go back to the litter. I gave her some food. We couldn't let any of the other cats near her. I fed them outside, on the driveway.

Saturday morning, with Blondie nursing the young, I locked the cage door. There were now four kittens with her. Joe and I took mother and litter to OHS. I gave the man at the desk my name. All the employees knew about Blondie, yes, she would be spayed on Tuesday. We could pick her up then. The litter would be put down painlessly. We left Blondie and litter and cage and went home.

Saturday evening I could feed the other four cats in the garage—Rusty, Sandy, Whitey and Randy. I had scheduled Sandy to be neutered on Monday. Both Sunday morning and Sunday evening, the cats came for their rations.

Sunday evening, at 11:00, I locked the garage door for the night. Inside were the four males. Monday morning, Joe let them out at 4:00 A.M., when he always moves our dog from inside the house where the canine spends the night,

At 6:10 I feed the cats, then go on to jog, etc. This morning, there were no cats. They had disappeared. I called them, but no cats came. It was strange. Later, just Sandy showed up. He was due at the vet between 8:00 and 9:00. I gave him his tranquilizer pill in a little food. After a half hour, I tried to put him in the carrier. He struggled fiercely and I had to let him go. Joe tried also. But the cat kept running and hiding. I went to Lenore and borrowed the OHS trap, took that into the garage and set it, Sandy wouldn't go in. It was useless. I called the vet and canceled the appointment. Too late anyway. I put away the trap and left food for Sandy, The tranquilizer had one effect. After he ate, Sandy fell soundly asleep and slept peacefully all day.

Then I went to look for Rusty. But, I thought, I already know what to expect. On my street, when a cat disappears, he doesn't return. He disappears "without a trace." Rusty and Whitey and Randy had disappeared. And Rusty and Randy already had been neutered.

I went from house to house. "Has anyone seen Rusty? He's deep orange." No one had. He and the other cats had vanished between 5:00 and 6:10 A.M. That's how long it took. Joe and I both felt bad.

"What's the use of neutering them if they are going to disappear? Let's at least spare them the trauma of the surgery."

At 2:30 one of my neighbors called. "I have Rusty. He's in my yard." When I ran to her house, there stood Sandy. However, later that evening, at about 5:30—surprise! Two cats ran into the garage and cried for food. They were Whitey, all covered with grease and with a hurt nose, and Randy. The only one missing was Rusty. We took hope from the fact that the three male teen-age kittens had come back. Toward evening, as the sun went down, Rusty appeared. We felt good about that. Rusty is a friendly cat, and he loves our dog, Lonesome.

Tuesday all went well with the animals. They experienced a slight trauma when Charlie, the handyman, responded to another call for help. Somewhere there was a leak in the washing machine plumbing. He came and checked everything out. "That trap (in the washer's drain) is corroded. You need a new one." Then he went out to buy the necessary part. He returned and substituted plastic for the rusty metal.

After that, he decided to replace some rotted wood in the frame of the garage back door. I had called him months before about the problem. With that door open, the cats ran out and hid. They returned when Charlie left. When I called OHS Tuesday to see if we could pick up Blondie on Wednesday, the answer was yes. But later, Lorraine of the facility called back to say that the vet could not be available for the spaying until Wednesday. Blondie would be released on Thursday. That was better because she would have more time to recover from the birth of the offspring and the milk would have dried up somewhat.

Thursday, Joe and I went to OHS with the cat carrier. The man at the desk asked if we had filled out a form. I said no, but I had spoken with the humane society director, and it was all right. I gave my name. Yes, he knew about me, but I would now have to fill out an adoption form. He had to authenticate my identity by checking my driver's license. Then he went into the surgery room with the carrier, advising the staff to get the cat.

When he came back, he gave me the bad news—a $40 adoption fee. That came as a surprise. The spaying was free, and the shots. I had not expected an adoption charge. Oh, well! I made out the check. Once again, he asked for my driver's license. Then he went to get Blondie. He came out with her in the carrier.

"I'd be careful with that cat if I were you. She's a little monster.

How could she be calm with all that had happened to her? "After all, she's a wild kitten."

Home we went with Blondie. When we put her into the garage, we opened the carrier. She climbed out cautiously. The other cats came up to examine her, And they hissed at her, Cats know each other by smell. Blondie didn't smell right. I was glad they didn't want anything to do with her. I wanted her to recuperate.

The vet must have done an exemplary job. Blondie climbed to the top of the cabinets in the garage and stayed there all day. I had prepared a bed for her with newspaper, in a covered litter box. She probably thought it too easily accessible by the other cats and the people. On high, she felt safe. And, in the evening, she jumped down. I worried that she would split herself open. After I fed them all, she ran outside. She stayed out all night and returned in the morning. I thought of all the warnings on the sheet we had received from OHS. "Keep her quiet; keep her where it is clean; check the incision to see if there is any infection." Try and keep her anything!

Now, at the time of this writing, more than a week later, Blondie is once more accepted by her siblings. She is lively and seems to be all right. She talks a lot, but I don't think she is in pain. And she loves Rusty.

I am trying to tame the cats. Rusty, of course, is pettable. The others allow various degrees of touch when they are eating—from Whitey, who jumps at my touch as though he has had an electric shock, to Sandy who purrs and continues to eat. They have made friends—some more than others—with Lonesome, who no longer barks at them. They will not multiply. But down the street, Lenore is feeding an unspayed female and her new fast-maturing litter. The problem is still there.

In the meantime, we have a cat circus with our "outside" cats. Our five "inside" cats are no trouble.

* * *

Eventually, we managed to trap first Sandy and then Whitey and take them to the vet. But that's another story.

1993

THE EIGHT THAT WALK

Our morning and evening walks with our dog, Lonesome, have taken many forms and been performed in a number of places. When he was a young dog, he jumped into the back of our square-back car and we drove to the industrial park for his journeys to relieve himself. As he became older, he could no longer manage the distance from the ground to the car platform. At first, Joe put the dog's front legs on the car and then boosted him up. As, with time, the canine became weaker, Joe lifted Lonesome bodily into the vehicle. This continued until my husband injured his back, necessitating a chiropractic visit. From then on, we made no more trips to the industrial park. We missed the little dog who had chased our car mornings and evenings during the years we had gone there.

In the meantime, we had adopted the five homeless cats who now live in our garage. And we have a new routine. At 4:30 in the morning, after he dresses, Joe opens the garage door, putting Lonesome out, and hooks our dog's leash to the door spring, When he does that, the five garage cats go out for their morning run.

It is still dark. I do not see them until after I wake up at 5:00, get dressed for jogging, eat breakfast, and prepare lunch. At 6:30 I jog, then seeing Lonesome and the cats.

These animals who spend their days and nights in the garage and an enclosure we had built attached to it, take advantage of their two-and-a-half hours of complete freedom. They race across lawns, chasing each other, climbing trees. Every now and then one darts out at me or follows for a short distance. It is still dark (winter) when I go out, but by the time I finish jogging, the sky has lightened.

Joe comes from the house, unhooks Lonesome and begins to take the dog for his walk. I join him. The cats know that when we return they will get their once-a-day canned cat food treat. They follow us, some for a short distance, a few for the entire walk. As we return, the ones who had dropped out join us. By the time we are halfway home, all five are with us, running in front or behind, or at the side of the road, keeping pace.

Sandy is the most companionable. He runs right in front of Lonesome who catches up and gives him a nudge as we go. We give

Sandy a pet. If Lonesome gets too familiar, the cat darts off, but returns immediately to accompany us.

Nearer the house we pick up Randy. He doesn't come too close to Lonesome, still not trusting the 75-pound dog. And then Whitey joins us at a respectable distance. Lonesome always lunges at Whitey, the only one of the five who is really afraid of him.

Still closer to the house, we are joined by Rusty and Blondie. The last 20 feet or so all five escort us, with Lonesome lunging at them, first to one side and then the other.

When we arrive home, the cats run into the building. Lonesome's leash is again hooked to the spring. He goes into the garage, but cannot reach the cats' feeding area. We close and lock the door.

I have already prepared their food. The cats get the canned contents; Lonesome gets to clean out the cans. He enjoys that, and he does a good job. After he is finished, Joe takes him into the back yard and lets him go free. The yard is fenced, and Lones has a doghouse. He gets water, a biscuit, and a slice of bread. He loves bread, At one time, the young dog had to be kept tied in the yard. He would dig under the fence or climb it to get out into the neighborhood. Since he is now old, his climbing and digging days are over.

The cats are secure for the day and night. After they have finished their canned food, they get the crunchies they will nibble all day. Once in a while, they may go through the pet port into the enclosure to get a little sun or to relieve themselves. But they are still semi-wild and uncomfortable in daylight, feeling safe only indoors and at night. They get up in the rafters, on the window screens and lumber we have stored there, or on the cabinets that line the garage wall, They liked to sleep on our air conditioning duct and on the hot water heater. However, because they couldn't resist doing their manicures on the insulation, Joe and I put a chicken wire barrier around the units. Up on high, the cats sleep in the daytime.

At night they come down and snuggle on the small braided rugs that I pulled up against the oil-filled radiator, plugged in for them during the winter. Or they go into the enclosure with the protection of darkness.

In my mind I can picture us and the six animals—Joe and me walking with Lonesome (Joe stopping to scoop up after the dog), escorted by five cats darting in front, behind, and beside us. As we make our way toward home, dawn gives way to daylight, And our morning stroll ends in the garage. The neighbors who happen to see us are amused.

1994

FURRY FUN

Our Jinny jumps onto my lap
And softly looks at me.
She's purring as I rub her neck;
She starts to knead my knee.

I lift her claws, then rub her nose-
She seems to understand
That I am offering my love;
She turns and licks my hand.

She sees me writing, lifts a paw
And tries to catch my pen;
I offer her the upper end-
She swipes at it again.

I say, "Why do you do that Jin?"
Her half closed eyes meet mine.
Her paws are fastened to the pen,
I cannot write a line.

She's purring, happy with her catch;
I want to author more.
I find another pen for her
And drop it on the floor.

She jumps down like a lightning streak
And gives that pen a fight;
I let her push her toy around,
And once more, I can write.

1994

TAMING BLONDIE

The little "garage cat," Blondie, is a distinct personality. She is the only non-male of the wild kittens. In addition to Rusty, the abused and abandoned adult, the males are Sandy, Randy, and Whitey. Rusty and Randy were neutered. Sandy and Whitey still need the surgery. Possibly one of them had impregnated Blondie, now spayed.

Do cats have feelings? Right away, it was obvious that Blondie loves Rusty. She keeps rubbing against him, sleeping with him. It was also apparent that she dislikes us. We are able to pet all the cats when they eat. But not Blondie. From the start, if a hand touched her, she jumped as though she was being given an electric shock.

Her eyes are perpetually round, making her expression one of surprise and suspicion. If Joe or I try to pet her, she meets our hand with an upraised paw. And the eyes seem to darken and get rounder.

I keep trying, sneaking a touch when she eats. Now she doesn't jump. But she still wants to get as far from me as possible–the farthest spot near the plate. And if she thinks I still will try to pet her, Blondie stops eating and takes a position some distance away, waiting for me to leave–or goes out through the pet port and sits outside on one of the boards that I had fastened horizontally to the chain link. Eventually, she does come in to eat.

Rusty likes to sleep on the washing machine. Blondie joins him. When I come into the garage, she jumps down immediately while Rusty remains to be petted. He reacts by purring, curling his paws and rolling. Rusty is a sweet cat. But then he never was wild. He had a home at one time.

When I made two carpeted eight inch wooden squares for the garage cats, Blondie immediately adopted them. When not sleeping with Rusty, she sits on one of the squares, enjoying the soft carpeting against her seat while she grooms herself.

We can't hold her unfriendliness against the little cat. She had no contact with people before we decided to feed her. And the visit to the vet didn't change her opinion of the two-legged animals.

Blondie has become an avid hunter, watching for lizards and roaches. We know from our previous experiences, that spayed females are the most dedicated predators.

Eventually, we hope to win her over. Until then, we continue to try petting her when she isn't looking. And hold the food until she is really hungry. At that time, she is most receptive to our touch. Taming Blondie will take a while. But persistence will win.

1994

JINNY'S DAY

Little Jinny follows me when I go into the back cat enclosure to scoop the litter area. First, she wants attention, rubbing on my legs until I pet her. And she looks me in the eyes to ask for more.

When I start to scoop, she tries to help me. As I dig, she digs with me, trying to grab the scoop with a dusty little paw. If I push some sand on her paws, if she feels I am being too rough–or if she tires of helping me, she runs off.

She likes to play with big dog Lonesome through the chain link of the enclosure. He is outside; she is in. Lones puts his nose to the fence. She reaches a paw through and tries to hit his nose. Jinny is ambidextrous–first one front paw, then the other. Sometimes Lones gets exasperated and snaps at the paws. But he never connects. Either he is pretending or Jinny is too fast. He never growls and rarely barks during this play.

Eventually, Jinny tires of all this activity. She climbs the wooden play "gym" that Joe constructed for the cats, and rests on the top plank. From that vantage point she can see the goings-on at the side front of the house. Or she decides that she is ready for her daily sleepy time. Then she jumps down, lies under an azalea bush where the shade is deepest. She still watches me with her eyes at half-mast. I finish my task and re-enter the house.

1994

A TALE OF CLAWS

On a Friday, our wild young cat, Mitty, was due at the vet. Mitty has extra toes on his front paws–mitten paws–Mitten, Mitty. The claws on the extra toes do not touch the ground. Instead, they curl under and into the paw pads. One vet called the problem "ingrown toe nails." Since Mitty is not tame enough to let these claws be trimmed periodically, removing them seemed the best solution to the problem. Even then, we put it off and put it off. We didn't want him to experience the trauma of going to the animal clinic. However, when he began to walk on three legs with one paw in the air, I decided, because Joe had other commitments, that I had to take him–my job.

He was suspicious when I brought the carrier into the Florida room and put it down near the food bowls which are usually in our cats' "apartment." He had not eaten since 7:30 the previous day, as the vet had requested, and he wanted his crunchies. The other cats had fasted with him. After a preliminary sniff at the carrier, they ran to the food. But Mitty looked at me and at the container and kept his distance. Finally, since the others were eating, he inched toward the bowls.

This was the moment I had been waiting for. I picked him up and put him, hissing and struggling, into the carrier. He howled and growled but I locked the lid. He acted entirely unlike his usual self, a timid non-violent little individual. I carried the container into the car. He yowled and continued to scold me all the way to the clinic. It was a relief to get there, take the carrier out of the car and bring it into the waiting room. With the motion, Mitty's protests stopped. He was quiet when the receptionist picked up the container and took him into the back room.

"Be careful," I cautioned her. No one knows what a wild animal– or even a pet animal–will do under stress.

"How did he behave?" I asked her when she returned.

"He growled at me. But he wasn't aggressive."

I left him there.

The next day, Saturday, at noon, when Joe and I went to pick him up, the receptionist was able to put him back into the carrier. We departed with the cat but left behind a sizeable amount of cash. The vet sold us an antibiotic and told us to keep Mitty in for a week so the paws wouldn't become infected.

Preparing for his isolation, we decided to put the little cat in the kitchen, a room that he knew. From it, he could look through sliding glass doors and see the other cats in the Florida room. I had prepared a litter box full of shredded newspaper, as the vet had suggested. I put down water, gave Mitty a cat napper–a circular bowl-shaped crocheted sleeping bed that my sister had made for a previous cat–and adulterated a little canned food with antibiotic, hoping he would be hungry enough after his fast to eat it. He ate ravenously. I added more food in the dish and a few of his favorite crunchies.

We went out for the afternoon. When we returned, he cried to be allowed into the Florida room with the other cats. It was time to feed them. They might as well eat together. When I removed the litter box and the cat napper from the kitchen, I noticed that Mitty had slept in the litter box. He had flattened the shredded paper,

I locked the pet port by inserting a "door," a piece of masonite that slides down through two channels on either side of the opening, Then I let the cats into the kitchen so they could be with Mitty.

Instead, Mitty ran to the pet port. He scratched at it and poked it with his sore paws. The other cats watched him as he meowed and tried to get out. And, in spite of the impossibility of lifting the masonite, he managed to get through the pet port and into yard, our "cat corral." I looked out and there he was, clawing at the ground and preparing it for an elimination. No wonder he acted so anxious to get out. The poor thing didn't know the purpose of a litter box. Well, so much for keeping his paws clean!

Mitty finished and covered up. I removed the barrier from the cat entrance, and he came in, ready to resume his relationship with his two favorite male cats, his buddies. They were his security blanket, his comfort. Usually, they groomed him and slept with him; they purred together and rubbed against each other in obvious demonstration of feline affection. Rut something had changed. Johnny and Jerry sniffed at Mitty, hissed at him, growled, and tried to bite him. Mitty was bewildered. He backed off and contented himself by eating a little and then settling down, hunched up, on the braided rug that the cats share in the Florida room. I realized that it was useless to attempt isolating him. So the litter box and the cat napper went into the garage and Mitty again was one of the bunch. We went out for the evening. On our return, Mitty was still–or again–hunched up by himself.

The next morning, I again gave Mitty some canned food with the antibiotic. Evidently, the medicine tasted good or was tasteless because he didn't object to it. After he finished, I gave him and the other four their usual morning meal. Again the two male cats growled and hissed when Mitty came up to them. And again they tried to bite him. They always attempt to bite an ear. One of the female cats, Jamie, repulses all the cats with this type of bite. Luckily Mitty's ears flatten when this aggression begins and the fangs meet nothing but air.

It took three days for the smell of the animal clinic or the medication to leave the little cat. I didn't give him the drug any more because his paws were healing. There was no infection. After that time, Johnny and Jerry once more nurtured their friend. And Mitty rubbed and purred and ate with them and slept with them.

Now he walks with confidence–before, he had almost tiptoed because of the claw problem. And if a cat can be called happy, Mitty is a happy little fellow. But he eyes me suspiciously. I still have to catch him off guard to give him a pet. Do-gooders seldom get thanked.

1994

QUINTET

Johnny chases Jinny;
Then she lies in wait for John.
Mitty plays at hiding,
While calm Jamie just looks on.

Jinny swipes at Mitty,
Who retaliates in kind;
Jerry's back end twitches
Like a spring set to unwind.

Back and forth they scamper,
Five young cats engaged in play;
I just stand and watch them
And their antics make my day.

1995

CANINE COMMUNICATION

I never cease to be amazed
    By canine repertoire-
A bark to warn a trespasser,
    "Stay, stranger, where you are";

A happy "woof" before a walk,
    A growl for things unknown;
A high-pitched whine for canine friends
    And for some cats (our own);

A yipe for hurt (an accident),
    When stepped on paw or tail;
A howl that means frustration, loss,
    Desire (to no avail).

This "talking," I appreciate.
    These are the sounds I hear,
He may make other sounds, their pitch
    Too high for human ear.

There is no voice for love or trust;
    I wonder if he tries
To make such sound, but there's no need-
    He says <u>that</u> with his eyes.

1995

MITTY SPEAKS

If Johnny eats from that one bowl,
It must have better food;
I'll push my head against his head;
We cats don't think it's rude.

I'll push him from those crunchy bits,
And eat what John ate too.
Hmm—tastes all right, but no big deal,
These crunchies; two will do.

Now, where's he going? He moved down;
He's eating from the next,
The other bowl. I'll try that too-
A head rub, my pretext.

The food in this one tastes the same.
It's boring. I should snooze.
He isn't on to something great-
Nothing I can't refuse.

I find a corner, start to doze-
Now here comes John; I purr.
He's finished eating, comes to me
And starts to lick my fur.

1995

EXIT WHITEY

We try not to show favoritism to any of our animals, but in spite of ourselves, we seem to give more attention to one or two.

This was the case with the five garage cats—Rusty, who had once had a home and been abandoned, and the four semi-wild felines who had come to live with us as teen-age kittens–Sandy, Randy, Blondie and Whitey.

Rusty became a favorite first. Having known a home, he responded to human friendship, rolling, purring, coming to us when he saw us. Of the wild kittens, first Sandy accepted our kindness. And then Whitey. Randy continued to be suspicious and Blondie absolutely refused to be friendly. Any attempt to give her a pet was countered with an upraised paw.

Perhaps, because of his color–an all-white blue-eyed cat among four felines in various shades of orange–Whitey received a little more attention than the others. He stood still to be petted and came to us whenever we were in the garage.

The other cats might have resented the attention that we bestowed on him. He always seemed to have a scratched nose. Being somewhat of a loner, he went through the pet port into the enclosure while the other cats slept on the rafters or cabinets. There, basking in the sun during the few winter hours that it warmed the area, he slept, coming in at 2:00 or 3:00 for food and petting.

Some evenings, after they returned from their feeding, when I opened the door from the garage into the house, Whitey or Randy or both, scooted into the living room. Randy, more than his friend, was apprehensive in this strange environment. He figured out that if he pushed against that door, it would open into the garage again, and he could escape, Whitey learned this trick too, but he was more interested in exploring the living room, although slightly edgy at first. Eventually, he didn't jump when we moved near him. And he could, on occasion, be petted.

Sunday morning, February 19, 1995, Whitey wasn't well. He stayed in the enclosure instead of joining the other cats in their morning walk to escort Lonesome. I mentioned this to our next-door neighbor. She was fond of Whitey. She said that some mornings, he ate with her cat, really friendly.

Sunday evening, he ate a few crunchies–or pretended to. Monday morning, Presidents' Day, he went out with the other cats. But he didn't return with them and Lonesome and us to the house.

I saved his food in the refrigerator. And all day, I made occasional trips to the front door to see if he had returned.

"He'll probably come back at dusk when he feels safe," we said. "He's probably sleeping somewhere, or was locked in someone's garage." But dusk came, and night. And Tuesday morning. Whitey had not come home.

I called my neighbor. "He ate with my cat Monday morning," she said. Well, that might explain why he had not returned that day with the other cats. He wasn't hungry. But where was he Tuesday?

"I'll let you know if I see him," she told me.

I made up some flyers and distributed them across the street and on both sides of my house.

All day Tuesday, we kept wondering what had happened to him. And Tuesday night came. Still no Whitey.

Wednesday morning, after we let the cats out for their few hours of freedom, my neighbor's son came to the house. "Your cat is dead," he said, "Whitey is in my flower bed. I thought he was sleeping, but he is stiff."

I went to look. He was dead, as Mike had said.

"I'd help you bury him, but I have to go to work."

"That's all right. Joe and I will take care of it." I petted the cold head of the little white body. My neighbor went toward his car. I started back toward our house.

Joe was just beginning to take Lonesome for his walk.

"Whitey is dead." Joe went to look. "I wonder what happened to him." There was no answer.

After Lonesome's walk; after the cats were locked in with their food; after the dog was brought to the back yard and given his biscuit—after the living felines were attended to, the four in the garage and the five in the Florida room—we took a paper bag from the kitchen and went to get Whitey. We buried him just outside the enclosure where he had slept in the sun. His spirit is probably still near the spot.

With so many animals, it is amazing how they become individuals who impress their personality on their human friends. I can see Whitey in the living room with his blue eyes looking at us. I can feel his fur, slightly rough—almost dog-like. And his generous tail, the end of the complete pet. And hear his purr.

Whitey is no longer with us. The four in the garage will now not be allowed to roam, Lonesome will spend nights inside our house. These cats will use the side enclosure for light and air and exercise. The five in the Florida room use the back enclosure.

Now we have a dog, Lonesome. And we have nine cats—Rusty, Sandy, Randy, Blondie, Jinny, Jerry, Jamie, Johnny, and Mitty.

1995

WALKING OUR DOG ON AN EARLY SPRING MORNING

It is still dark, pre-dawn;
The air, cool and clean—
Humidity down;
The road crunches underfoot;
And Lonesome plods ahead,
A weary old dog.

1996

JINNY'S QUANDARY

Now, five cats in the Florida room, four J's and Mitty. The oldest "J" is Jinny; then Jerry, Jamie and Johnny.

One day, as I watched through the sliding glass doors from the kitchen, I saw that Jinny's favorite chair was usurped by Johnny and Mitty who cuddled together to stay warm, Jinny also liked the wooden "park bench" we gave them and slept on it when her chair was taken.

But today the bench also was occupied. On the plastic-covered cushions that are on the slats, lay Jerry and Jamie, one at each end of the bench. In the center the two cushions come together, forming a ridge.

Jinny sat on the floor in front of the bench and looked first at Jerry and then at Jamie and then again at the two sleeping cats. The only spot available was in the center on the ridge. She jumped on the little table that stands at one end of the bench and looked down at Jerry. If she snuggled against him, there would be room for her. But Jerry and Jinny are not special friends. Jinny looked and pondered on the situation; then she jumped to the floor.

I went in.

"Do you want a place to sleep, Jinny?"

In the Florida room we had put the cabinet that used to hold a wall oven. We added a shelf inside the opening, above the two drawers. And we laid a plastic-covered cushion on the shelf. I picked up Jinny and put her on the cushion.

Jinny had never slept on that shelf. It was usually Jamie's refuge, but now Jamie was on the bench. Jinny sniffed the cushion and looked around the enclosed space. Then she came to a decision. No, not her kind of sleeping space. She jumped down and went back to the bench, again looking up from side to side. She seemed to measure the distance between Jamie and Jerry.

Something distracted me and I left my watching spot for a few minutes. When I returned, Jinny was between the other two cats, sleeping on the ridge where the two cushions butted together. And about an hour after that, both Mitty and Johnny were at the cat bowls, eating. And Jinny was curled up on her favorite chair. Jinny had won out by default.

1996

THE GARAGE CATS AND THE MILK

Randy came in from the side enclosure. In the garage he saw the little dish of milk I had left there. He began avidly to lap up the milk. Sandy came up. He didn't know what Randy was drinking, but if it was good he wanted some. He lifted a paw and feinted a blow. Randy retreated. Sandy sniffed the milk and decided he didn't like it. He left to eat some crunchies from the dry food bowl.

Randy went back to the milk, and lapped it busily. Blondie came in through the pet port. She noticed Randy's activity and came near the dish, but kept a short distance from the male. Blondie is afraid of a confrontation, being smaller than the others.

She waited. And waited. And waited. Finally, her patience was rewarded. Randy, satiated, walked away from the milk. Blondie edged up to the dish and began to lap up the treat.

1996

SPAT

Blondie likes Rusty. He doesn't bother her, even though he is a male (neutered), while both Sandy and Randy have enough male hormone to go through mating preliminaries.

Outside, in their enclosure, I watched Blondie flirt—if she were human, that would be the word—with Rusty, She rubbed against him, groomed him by licking his face and head, and then repeated her attentions.

Rusty took it for a while. Then he responded to her activity by becoming male. He tried to nip her neck fur and then imprison her with his front paws. This turn of events surprised the little female. They scuffled; she spit at him.

Then, followed by Rusty, she ran through the pet port into the garage. Spat ended, both settled down to a few crunchies and then their usual naps.

1996/7

SICK CAT

Our little white cat, Mitty, had a problem. Now and then he would cry out and try to get away from himself, his eyes big and black. Joe thought something bit him. When he ate, he pulled the food out with his paw and licked the morsel off. It seemed as though he couldn't bend his head down and eat directly from the plate the way the other cats did. And he became thin. I could feel his vertebrae when I petted him.

I made an appointment with the veterinarian, but I couldn't keep it. When Mitty saw the carrier, he spit at me and growled. After all, he had been a wild kitten.

Two weeks went by, and it was obvious that he was experiencing sharp and sudden pain. Sometimes he lifted a paw to his jaw and clawed at his mouth. I had to get him to the vet. On Friday, the 21st of June, 1996, I went to the clinic and spoke with the two girls at the desk. I would pay someone to get Mitty into the carrier. But neither could leave the premises. I decided to go right to the Orlando Humane Society and see what they could do. We were long-time members.

The people at the OHS know me. I explained the problem. Dean could do it, they said. They called him. He was at the airport. Dean was the OHS cruelty investigator. He had been at our house before, when we had the awful wild cat multiplication problem. Yes, Dean would come directly from the airport.

He came at 4:00. The vet clinic closes at 5:00. Mitty spit and growled at him the way he had at me. It was obvious that no one could pick him up. Dean used a snare at the end of a pole to get Mitty around the middle. Screaming and struggling, Mitty was dumped into the carrier. The other four cats in the Florida room went wild also, as I had locked the pet port to keep Mitty from escaping into the enclosure.

I was starting to prepare dinner so Joe took the carrier to the vet. At almost 6:00 Joe returned with the cat. Mitty had calmed down a little, but was still spitting when we approached.

Joe told me what happened. When Mitty was released from the carrier at the animal clinic, he screamed and ran around the room. Dr. Tolliver used a snare, this time getting Mitty around the neck. Once the man and assistant captured the cat, the doctor gave him an injection. The little animal went out like a light.

"He doesn't look like a sick cat to me," commented Joe.

"He's sick, all right," said the vet.

Mitty had two badly infected teeth. Dr. Toliver extracted them and gave him an antibiotic injection. While Joe was there I called to say that since Mitty was still under the anesthetic, he might as well have all his shots, including the one for leukemia.

The vet suggested that Mitty remain in the carrier overnight. Home the patient went. We thought he would rest quietly in what is now the computer room. When we looked in and talked to the little cat, he spit. The next morning, Joe brought the carrier into the Florida room and opened it. Mitty walked out slowly, looking around to make sure that he was home; then shot out through the pet port, into the enclosure.

After he recovered from his ordeal, he was able to eat. He gained a little weight. But the improvement was temporary. He should have his teeth cleaned every six months, the vet told us. When he began to cry at the food dish, we had to take him. A friend came to put him into the carrier, using heavy gloves. But Dr. Tolliver still snared him. We vowed never again.

OHS said they would do his teeth, and no snares. Then we bought a squeeze cage to hold him while the anesthetic was administered through the openings. He could be put out before being removed from the cage. But that is another story.

1997

FAREWELL, LONESOME

Today, March 26, 1997, our dog, Lonesome died. Last week he had a bath and a dip. The week before he had been clipped. This morning we walked him. And this evening. Tonight, he ate his usual portion of dog food.

About 8:00 P.M. he started making strange coughing sounds. And mucous came up—thick white foam. I petted his head. Then he indicated that he wanted to go out. Joe took him for a walk. He had a bowel movement and Joe brought him back into the house. But the coughing continued. Again he wanted to go out. Suddenly, it rained. Joe put on the slicker and again went with Lones. A few minutes later, Joe came back. Our dog was lying in the grass, not breathing. He was dead.

Joe couldn't control his grief. He took some plastic sheeting from the garage and covered the rain-soaked body. Later, we both pulled Lones from the grass onto the driveway. Tomorrow, Joe will bury him.

I have so many memories of him. First, as an abandoned dog, thin, with matted fur dangling on both sides of his face. How he stayed in our yard occasionally, angering me because he wanted to dig himself a bed under the azaleas. He looked as though he needed a friend. I called him "Lonesome." Then, how he gave me a sharp look as I came out of the house with scissors and flopped at my feet to let me cut off the matted hair.

How he refused dog food, but occasionally ate a slice of bread from my hand.

How he jogged with me but at a safe distance and became possessive if someone came near me.

Then, how desolate he looked when animal control, called by a neighbor because he had barked at her daughter, put him in the truck. And how we decided that evening to get him.

How, when we first put him in the garage, he thought we had trapped him. He clawed at the door trying to get out. Eventually, he realized that he would be freed when day arrived.

How we left a square dance in a thundershower because we had tied him on a long lead under a tree in the yard. We put him in the garage. A week later he had a dog house.

How he jogged with me when he became our dog, on a leash after he detoured to chase cats, squirrels, bicycles, trucks and an occasional pedestrian.

How, when he was being treated for heartworms, Joe took him for a walk and Lonesome collapsed. Joe walked home, then took the car and we both drove to where Lonesome lay. We lifted the prostrate dog into it and drove home.

How Joe decided to take him to the industrial park mornings and evenings to let him run free and take care of his needs. He didn't dirty in the house. And how Joe cried as he called me from the vet after a truck hit Lones and nearly killed him. The vet called him a miracle dog.

How he could sniff out chicken bones from a distance, no matter how old they were, covered with ants. He lost no time chomping on a discarded bone. Those were the only times I hit him.

How, in the house, evenings, he put his head on my lap as I watched TV or read.

How, as time went on, he became weaker. He could no longer jump into the back of the station wagon. Then Joe began to give him a boost, putting the front paws on the car deck and then lifting his hind quarters. And later, how Lones couldn't even do that. Joe lifted him bodily into the car.

How, when it became too difficult for Joe, we began walking Lones on our block, in the street, mornings and evenings. The neighbors knew him and us. Joe carried a coal scoop and a sheet of newspaper to pick up after him.

I think of how Lonesome received little attention, except for the times we walked him. In the evening, when it rained, he was confined to the kitchen, while we went about our various activities. We could not leave him in the living room after he had had a few "accidents." And we had given the garage to the four of our nine cats.

In the daytime, we fenced him in our back yard, where he had grass, shade and water. He had the company of ducks who wandered up from the canal. And he could share the chain link of the cat enclosure with the five Florida room cats.

When Lonesome and Joe walked, they progressed slowly, Lonesome wanted to sniff at everything. And he would wet here and there. On garbage collection days, the going was especially slow. Joe said, "Lonesome knows the world with his nose." Probably, our dog was looking for chicken bones. He paid special attention to the street drain. I don't know what odor came up from it.

I remember how, when we walked, often Lonesome acted in a manner that could have been only a show of affection. He bonked his head hard against my hand or Joe's. I called it "purring." He would do it a number of times in succession. And many times, to get close, he would step on my foot, or Joe's. And our "nice doggie, good doggity," would be accompanied by "get off my foot." He weighed 65 pounds. Without him, we can walk fast, unhampered by the dog who knew the world with his nose. But something irreplaceable has gone out of our lives.

I recall how frustrated I was on Halloween in 1995, when our doorbell kept ringing and our "guard dog" didn't make a peep even though I pushed him toward the door and barked to show him what he should do.

And how, when he came in contact with the cats, he was one of them—the dog and the cats sleeping together and grooming each other.

The last year he couldn't always wait for his walks, and we had to clean up the stool. But he never wet in the house.

When we went on trips, we put him in a kennel. The people there loved him. But he was always happy to see us again.

Now it's over. Our only dog is gone. He shared our lives for 15 years. In the book, "Across the Line", which Anice Terhune, via automatic writing, attributes to her late husband, Albert Payson Terhune, he says, "the dogs are with me." According to Terhune, the souls of animals also "cross the line." Lonesome, auf wiedersehn.

1998

WATCHING MITTY

From the kitchen we can look through sliding glass doors into the Florida room, home of five of our nine cats. Cat watching is fun.

Today, Jerry, the grey tiger cat, is preparing to eat some of his dry food. Mitty comes up to see what Jerry is eating. Jer lifts a paw and pushes Mitty's head. Mitty leaves. Jer decides he doesn't want the food after all. While he is still near the bowl, the little white cat comes back. This time Jerry has decided that the other cat is okay. He holds Mitty's head with a paw and licks him.

Mitty sees that Johnny, the long-haired orange cat, is eating the canned food. Mit thinks he might like some. But John's head is covering the entire dish. Mitty reaches out a paw and tries to remove a particle from under Johnny's nose. John ignores him and Mit gives up. John finishes and exits through the pet port. Jerry goes out too. Mitty wonders why they have gone out, but maybe it's a good idea. He starts for the pet port but thinks better of it. He goes back to the plate of canned food.

He puts a left front paw into the plate, pulls out a morsel, and licks it from his paw. He continues to eat this way for a few minutes, He also pulls a few chunks out with his mouth and eats them from the floor.

Eating this way takes a long time. For perhaps ten minutes he pulls out particles. He probably considers this way of eating good manners and can't understand why John put his face down on the plate. Mit uses his left paw–a southpaw.

He goes around the plate and checks the tray on which it stands to see if he missed any morsels. Then he examines the floor around the tray. He manages to find a few crumbs. One chunk fell outside the tray and almost under it. Mitty tries to coax it out. Finally, using his right paw, he is able to get it away from the tray. Now he eats it. He finishes his meal and leaves through the pet port.

1998

MITTY'S ORDEAL

Mitty is back home asleep in his squeeze cage. Joe, wearing the heavy welder's gloves, had captured him screaming and struggling, and pushed him into the cage to take him to the Orlando Humane Society. His teeth had been bothering him, and he was due for his semi-annual cleaning, A feral cat, he could not be picked up, could not be coaxed into the cage, could not be treated by the veterinarian unless he was completely sedated. We agonized over the ordeal, but it was necessary; he has congenitally bad teeth, some pulled, subject to cavities and infections.

But now it is a few days later. He is back in his cage in the Florida room, sleeping soundly. The cage is a wire mesh contraption, horizontal wires spaced an inch apart, vertical wires two inches apart. Inside is a separate panel of wires, with some extending through the cage, forming handles. When these are pulled, the inside panel moves toward the side of the cage, forcing the occupant against it, The veterinarian can give the patient a shot through the openings in the wire mesh. We bought it for Mitty.

What went through Mitty's head through the entire teeth-cleaning process? We can only guess. He was forced, struggling, into the cage. Then, in the safety of that cage, which he knew, transported to the humane society building, not uncomfortable in the car. He probably remembered that he had come home previously from a similar trip. He yowled a few times. Then Joe, who had taken him, removed the cage with Mittty inside and brought it into the building. For a while, Mitty, still protected by the cage, lay in the waiting area. A dog came near. The feline spit and tried to claw the canine. The dog retreated.

What else does Mitty remember? Eventually, someone picked up the cage. He probably spit and howled. After being jabbed with something sharp, he now was home with a bad taste in his mouth, still in the protective cage. For a few hours he rested, sleepy (under the influence of the anesthetic). Then he awoke, groggy. After another hour or so, we allowed him out of the cage. The poor little thing fell when he tried to walk. He kept trying, staggering,

The cage was still where we had brought him, but Mitty wanted to be with the other cats, back in the Florida room. He tried to pry the sliding glass door open. Eventually, someone opened it, and he tottered into the room. Because he acted strange and smelled strange, his friends spit at him. He went through the pet port into the outside enclosure.

The people at the OHS had folded a large towel under him to absorb his urine. I put the towel in a plastic bag and took it outside. On collection day, it would go to the landfill. I swabbed out the cage with a damp paper towel and a little detergent. Then I dried it with another towel and set it in the Florida room. I added a little catnip. Cat Jerry went into the cage for the treat. Johnny sat outside the cage, waiting for his turn.

Mitty stayed in the enclosure all night. Still wobbly; he felt safe, distanced from his spitting friends. The next day he came back through the petport and drank a little water. That afternoon, he was back in his cage.

It is now almost a week later. He has eaten and had something to drink each day after the first. What had he experienced? A fight with Joe, a ride in the car, a wait in the reception area, a strike at a curious dog, a slight hurt from something jabbed into him, home with that bad taste. The whole time he had been safe in his cage. So Mitty again sleeps there.

1998

INSTINCTS

Unlike the human animal who must learn everything from other people or the four-footed beasts, the latter have been preprogrammed to do what they do, even though they have never learned from another one of their own kind.

The instinct to hunt and how to hunt has been built in by nature. Herbivores have their own instincts that tell them what to eat and what not to eat. Since our own contacts have been limited to dogs and cats, I have observed some of the idiosyncracies of our pets.

From the bedroom window, I watched Jinny prepare to relieve herself. In the back enclosure–one of cat corrals–she looked around, trying to find a clean spot. Nature had told her to go under some bushes for privacy. But it had been raining each day; the ground had become hard. Under the bushes, an occasional drip had reprogrammed Jinny. She didn't want to get wet.

She found an appropriate spot on the grass. No need to dig. She passed her stool. Now she must cover up. But she doesn't know that. She had the need to scratch the area near the elimination. She didn't turn around. Almost exactly where she had stood, she began to scratch– near the front of her length, below her chin, instead of to the rear.

After tearing up some turf, she turned, as instinct told her, and sniffed. The smell was still there. She clawed at the grass again. But to one side of the stool, not at the source of the odor. She sniffed again. Then, apparently satisfied or discouraged, she went back to the concrete patio to take a nap.

In the garage, we placed two litter boxes. The four garage cats have a smaller outside area in which to take care of their needs. And when it rains, their outdoors is wet, very wet. Therefore, the litter boxes.

The same instinct that causes cats to dig and go through the motions of covering up, applies to litter boxes. Sandy and Blondie prefer the boxes while Rusty and Randy go outdoors.

I watched Sandy. He likes to wet in the litter box as well as eliminate in it. He ruins the litter–the clay doesn't dry, especially in humid weather–which is most of the time. Sandy went into the box, not wanting to make a depression for his necessities. Evidently, he didn't like to dirty his paws. I always put the litter box on a number of newspaper sheets. Sandy climbed out of the box, sniffed at his product, and then scratched at the newspapers. He went around the box, sniffing, but he never put his paws into the box. He shredded the newspaper. At least once a week, I replace the paper. The litter box is scooped at least three times a week, sometimes daily.

Blondie uses the other litter box. I watched her. She doesn't urinate in the box. She scratched the litter to make a depression. She produced a dry stool, clawed the litter around it, rearranging the clay, not covering the elimination. She sniffed; then out of the box she went, but not entirely. She balanced on the rim, stirring up the litter with one paw. Enough–she jumped completely off the box and scratched the newspaper.

Cats have the instinct to dig and then cover up. It is interesting to see what deviations nature allows their limited capabilities.

1998

MITTY'S DILEMMA

Mitty, the white cat with the extra toes, came into the Florida room through the pet port. The sudden transition from outside to inside seemed to daze him. He turned around and sat a foot away from the port, staring at the entry.

Then he evidently accepted the fact that he was in the house. He found a spot on the braided rug and settled on it, scrunching himself into a turtle-like mass.

A moment later he went to the food bowl, consuming a few morsels, It was as if he thought, "since I am near the food, I might as well have a little."

I turned away for a minute. When I looked again, he was nowhere to be seen. He had made his exit through the pet door, probably deciding that outside was better and wondering why he had come in at all.

1998

ANOTHER CAT TALE

Among the garage cats, Randy, the only adventurous one, comes into the living room occasionally when we open the garage-to-living room door. If I hold the door open and call him, he doesn't respond. But if he wants to come in, he zooms through the opening. Then he does a little investigating of the living room, the kitchen and the hall. He sits, rolls on the soft carpet, and grooms himself. The other rooms are closed off. The carpets in the living room, dining area and study are periodically treated with Pestex for fleas, This started when Lonesome shared our home.

Still, Randy is uneasy. He is basically a wild cat. In the garage, he lets me pet him, but not in the house. I leave the entry door to the garage unlocked. Randy has discovered that he can push the door open and escape into familiar territory when his explorations have ended. The other three cats, with the exception of Rusty who came in once or twice, are satisfied to remain in the garage and the attached outside enclosure.

The Florida room cats all want to come into the house proper. Once in a while, we forget to close the sliding door and they rush in, spreading out in all directions. We round them up and put them back. Five are too many at one time. And grey tigercat, Jerry, is still enough of a male to squirt when he is in strange territory.

In the evening, now that Lonesome is gone, we let little orange Jinny into the living area from 8:00 to 11:00. Jerry, the squirter, is not allowed. Mitty, the white male, is too timid; as is Jamie, the peaceful orange female. Then there is Johnny.

Jinny is the most people-oriented. She comes to Joe and me to be petted. She purrs and rubs and gives our hands an occasional lick. She sits near me in the study on another chair and watches TV, or beside me on the sofa as I read.

Sometimes, when I open the sliding door to let Jinny in, Johnny runs in with her. Johnny is the long-haired cat, rescued from starvation by my neighbor. I also call him "Fluffy" or "F'uffy." He is friendly to a point. But cautious. When coming into the living room, he rolls and stretches on the carpet. John investigates the nooks and crannies of the unfamiliar area, doing a lot of talking. But he cringes when we want to pet him. And he tries to escape. After an hour or so, he meows continuously. It is time, he lets us know, for his return to the security of the Florida room. We open the sliding door and let him into his familiar surroundings.

One evening, for some reason, I opened the door that leads from the living room to the garage. John, who had been following me, darted through the opening.

"Uh oh," I thought, "we are going to have a confrontation."

Only Randy sat in the garage. The other three orange cats–Rusty, Sandy and Blondie, were in the enclosure. Randy prepared to do battle with the intruder.

Johnny ignored his half-brother–both had been born to the same mother. The fluffy one began to explore the garage.

Randy followed with his eyes. I watched, waiting to rescue Johnny if a battle ensued.

Fluffy continued his exploration. Then Randy thought it was time to make his presence and attitude more obvious. He howled.

I called Johnny, but he was still poking his nose into all the nooks in this fascinating new world. He didn't respond to Randy's challenge, and he didn't come to me.

I wanted to avoid warfare. I went to F'uffy, picked him up and returned to the living room. Moments later, he asked to go back into his Florida room haven.

All this time Jinny, in the living room, had been sitting quietly at Joe's feet as he watched his TV program.

1999

BLONDIE OUTSIDE

Our outside cat, Blondie, is one of the four cats who shared the garage. Originally, we had five, but Whitey died, killed by our neighbor—our late neighbor. Rusty, the older cat, had been abused and abandoned. The other four, Whitey, Sandy, Randy, and Blondie, were feral kittens, born on our street. The four were fathered by a Siamese. Their mother, Mandy, an abandoned long-hair, now spayed and adopted two houses down, had other litters, brought to the humane society or animal control. These four—and Rusty—became our cats when they were befriended by our dog. We called them our garage cats, closed in, with a pet port to an outside enclosure. We did let them out mornings until Whitey died. Then the garage served as their permanent home.

The three remaining males were neutered and Blondie spayed. Due to delays by the humane society, the little female, almost a kitten herself, had a litter. The new-borns and mother went to the OHS together. The mother returned; the litter didn't.

For a while, the four cats lived peaceably in the garage. When our dog shared their space, they considered him their mother, kneading and purring and going through feeding activity. Lonesome, the dog, tolerated their attention and patiently accepted their friendship.

Lonesome died; now four cats shared the garage. Sandy somehow forgot that he had been neutered. He began to display male cat characteristics, spraying and trying to mate with Blondie. Sometimes he attacked Randy, and sometimes Rusty. Rusty, equal to the occasion, flipped on his back and defended himself with all four paws. Randy, almost as heavy as Sandy, sometimes retaliated. But poor Blondie became a continual victim.

When we heard a ruckus in the garage, we went in and broke up the confrontation. But when we were not home, poor Blondie suffered. She became so paranoid that she would not go to the outside enclosure through the pet port. If she went through, Sandy followed her, making a pest of himself. So Blondie could not use the outside litter area. We found droppings at various spots in the garage—on the washing machine, on the bicycle seats, on the electric saw bed, in corners. We could tell, of course, that she had defecated. The smell was a give-away. Then I would have to find the stool and clean it up. Also, the puddles of her urine and the spray from Sandy.

We had had it. We decided to put Blondie out. She would be our outside cat. Using his thick welder's gloves, Joe managed to grab her. I had opened the door from the garage to the living room and from the living room to outdoors. Blondie, released, ran through like a streak.

Now, in the garage, no more spraying, no more stools, no more puddles. Sandy attacked Randy occasionally, but most of the time, the three males snuggled against each other and behaved peaceably. Blondie roamed our property, returning to our front porch for her food. By this time our cat-killing neighbor had died, and we were optimistic that Blondie would survive.

We had two oil-filled electric radiators in the garage for winter weather. When the cold winds blew, we brought one of the radiators outside to the porch. Blondie discovered the heat and rested on top of the radiator when the temperature dropped into the 40's and 30's. We had fastened a metal mesh to the top of the radiators, making a level surface. On this we placed a thick wad of aluminum foil and a folded towel.

Blondie was comfortable underneath, but above and around her the winter winds blew. We tried to get her into the house, but, being a feral cat, she didn't trust us. So we decided to put a house around her. We closed in the porch with doors installed at both ends and cutouts so that Blondie could enter and leave from either side. The radiator heated the enclosed porch, and without the wind, the entire area became comfortable.

Blondie liked her new home. She adopted the little table and two plastic chairs I had placed inside, with a crocheted cat napper on one chair. She liked the napper when the weather became more clement. I put her food and water bowls inside the enclosed area. And life became easier for people and cats.

Then came a fly in the ointment. A stray male cat discovered the porch and the food. He decided that it was better to be fed than hungry. So now, when I fed Blondie, I had to sit with her until she finished. But, feeling sorry for the male cat, now dubbed "Big Boy," I made up another bowl of crunchies and put it outside the enclosed porch area.

Mornings and evenings, Big Boy came for his rations. However, he liked Blondie's food better, so I still had to sit with her until she finished. Then, with her bowl back in the kitchen, Big Boy had no alternative but to eat from his. If his food remained outside until dark, a possum came by to finish what he left.

This is all a preliminary to Blondie's story. We are always amazed by her astuteness. Being a feral cat, she is afraid of people. She is afraid of cars. But she knows ours. The little cat comes out to welcome us as we pull into the driveway. She runs when strangers walk toward our door. She decided that the mailman was harmless; knowing that he goes to the house, leaves the mail and returns to his truck at the curb, never deviating from his route or showing a sign that he has noticed her.

Blondie is afraid of Big Boy and keeps out of his way. However, he has never bothered her or tried to mate with her. His aggressiveness is limited to the crunchies. Blondie also tolerated the possum. I had bought inexpensive cat food for the rodent. He has since died.

Blondie likes to eat a few crunchies, go outside for a little stroll, and come back for a few more bites. And she won't eat until she gets petted. Feeding her takes time. My rewards are a rub and a purr. These from a formerly feral cat who jumped when she was touched.

Her face has lost the scowl she had in the garage. She is no longer covered with scratches. Every now and then she becomes frisky and races across the lawn. She doesn't climb, although we have two trees in the front yard and three in the back. When I do any yard work, she follows me. If the work involves digging or planting, she investigates the new development, sniffing the spot. I call her my helper. When my work is finished and I return to the house, she goes back into her porch—her house.

The garage cats know that she is outside. They try to see her from the space under the doors. Sometimes she and they engage in a game of pat-a-cake. Sometimes Blondie goes to the front gate of their enclosure. And through the chain link a battle develops, three cats, inside, growling and snarling at the one outside.

The emerging of Blondie's personality shows what can happen if an animal is given the freedom to develop. To a lesser extent, our other eight cats display their own uniqueness.

THE NINE CATS

THE NINE CATS

THE FLORIDA ROOM CATS:

Jinny, an orange female, weighing perhaps seven pounds. Found walking two streets from ours in 1989. She must have been six months old at the time.

Jerry, a grey male tigercat, about 18 pounds. Adopted from the Orlando Humane Society in 1990. He must have been a year old at the time,

Jamie, an abandoned orange female, about 12 pounds. Had a litter in a neighbor's garage. Adopted in 1992. She was probably less than a year old at the time.

Johnny, a long-haired orange male, about 14 pounds. Found starving by a neighbor. He must have been about three months old at the time. Adopted in 1992. His mother, an abandoned longhaired female.

Mitty (Mittens), white blue-eyed male with extra toes, about 10 pounds. Problems with teeth. Same mother as Johnny. Father, an abandoned Siamese. Was a feral kitten. Adopted 1993.

THE NINE CATS, continued

THE GARAGE CATS:

Rusty, deep orange male, about 18 pounds. Probably the father of Johnny. Abused and abandoned. He must have been about 2 years old when we adopted him in 1993.

Sandy, feral orange male with white bib and paws, about 18 pounds. Same mother as Johnny and Mitty. Father, Siamese. He was a kitten when adopted in 1993.

Randy, (also Brandy). Pale orange—peaches and cream—male, about 16 pounds, with white bib and paws. Also extra toes. Horizontal ears. Same mother as Johnny and Mitty, littermate of Sandy. Adopted 1993.

THE OUTSIDE CAT

Blondie, petite orange female, about 6 pounds. Littermate of Sandy and Randy. Adopted 1993.

2000

BLONDIE AND THE CARS

After 30 years of used cars (Joe couldn't stand the thought of the instant depreciation when a new car is taken from the dealer), we decided we had had it with all the problems associated with someone else's headache, In 1997, both Joe and I bought new cars—his, a Honda; mine, a Hyundai.

Now, it was time for a 2000 model. Joe had over 30 thousand miles on the Honda. And he had just had our first large bill for service. "Time for a new car, Joe." He thought about it; then decided to see what was available in station wagons. We had owned a car with that type of body since we drove Lonesome, to his destinations.

Joe researched Saturns on the internet; and finding a model that he liked, decided to trade in the Honda on the Saturn. We received a quote on a trade-in. The amount was acceptable, and the deal was done. On the appointed day we drove home in the new vehicle.

Blondie knows our cars. Most days, when the Honda was in the driveway, she slept under it. She is protected from the hot sun and from any dog or other animal that might challenge her. If another car drives up, she runs into the neighbor's yard, under his inoperable van, which decorates that driveway. But she preferred the Honda. And, that away, she slept under the Hyundai.

Blondie recognizes our cars. When we drive up toward the house, she comes to welcome us, but stays well out of the way until the motor is turned off. When a strange vehicle pulls up, she runs and hides. She knows they are not ours.

The day we drove home in the Saturn, the little cat came to greet us as usual. But the noise of the car sounded strange. She stopped in her tracks, undecided whether to come toward us or run. Then, on short legs, she started for the neighbor's yard. Joe called to her.

"Here, Blondie. Here, Blondie." He went toward her, intending to pet her. But she continued to the next yard, looking back over her shoulder occasionally to see if she was being followed.

We laughed, and Joe gave up trying to bring her back. We went into the house.

The next day, Blondie had evidently decided that the Saturn was okay. And she now sleeps under the new car, as she had under the previous one. She even sits on the hood as she had with the Honda and surveys the world from on high.

2000

BLONDIE AND FRIEND

Jogging in the morning, I get the chance to watch Blondie, our outside cat, in her wanderings. She has just finished the food I have given her. I sat with her until the stray cat, Big Boy, finished his breakfast and wandered off. Now, I don't have to protect her from him.

Blondie likes to cross the street. Fortunately, there is little traffic on our dead-end block. And Blondie is afraid of cars. But she likes to explore the yard of the neighbor on the other side of the road.

A few days ago, as I watched while I jogged past, she started to make her customary dash across the blacktop. This time, following her at a distance of about four feet, was a small bird. Blondie scampered; the bird hopped. The bird kept the same distance between them all the way, until Blondie reached the other side

Blondie realized she was being followed. She stopped, turned, and stared at the tiny feathered one. The bird stopped also and stared back. Then Blondie resumed her trip through the neighbor's yard.

The bird did not follow.

2000

BEWILDERED MITTY

Accidentally, in the Florida room, replenishing their water and food bowls, I stepped on Jerry's paw. Mitty, who heard Jerry cry, ran out through the pet port. Jer, knowing that I do not hurt him intentionally, is forgiving. He remained by the food. I went to get more.

A second later, Johnny came in. He and Jerry were both now at the food bowls. I brought more crunchies. While I was in the Florida room, Mitty came back. He looked at me with eyes like saucers; then at Jerry and Johnny, now eating peacefully; then at me, and again at them. One more time, he checked me out, his eyes less frightened.

He stayed in the Florida room, but close to the pet port. After I left, he joined the other two cats at the food.

2000

RANDY'S TOY

Early morning–I went into the garage, and then the side enclosure, to get replacement water for the two bowls always available to the three males. Rusty sat high on one of the boards I have fastened to the chain link; Sandy, indoors, slept on the mesh Joe had nailed between some garage beams. Randy, in the enclosure, was absorbed in something. I looked more closely.

Randy pounced. Perhaps he had a lizard that needed rescuing. No, his victim was a grasshopper. Randy took the bug in his mouth and carried it to his "lair," the concrete block area closer to the house wall. He dropped the insect and watched it,

The grasshopper began to crawl. Randy waited. Then the bug hopped, Randy made a lightning jump and again imprisoned it in his mouth. He carried it back to his previous location.

Should I rescue the insect? Usually, when I see a hopper in the garden I go for the insecticide spray. No, the bug didn't seem to be damaged. I wanted to see Randy's next move, deciding to give him one more fling before I took the grasshopper from him.

Again the victim began to crawl. And once more the cat waited. A hop and a pounce. Back to square one.

"OK, bug, I'll give you your freedom. Randy will have to find another toy." Now, how to pick it up?

Before I could figure out how to grab it, the insect crawled out of the enclosure and into the neighbor's yard. Randy didn't bother it. He was interested in his toy only if it hopped.

Grasshoppers do a great deal of damage to a garden. Randy's toy escaped a premature demise.

THE INSPECTOR

Almost every day I do some garden work. Mostly it involves weeding. Sometimes I transplant a stray purslane into a more pleasing area, Sometimes I dig up a dead bush or remove a flowering plant that has outlived its appeal.

Invariably, I am followed by our outside cat, Blondie. The little orange female is interested in what I am about. She watches to make sure I am doing everything right, standing by me, and perhaps wondering why I am bent over in a seemingly useless task when I could be petting her. And she goes with me to the weed bag, sniffing for enticing aromas.

After I finish, Blondie returns to the last worked-on site. She inspects my job, puts her nose near everything, touches the soil here and there to ascertain if it is suitable for a litter area. Sometimes she decides the moisture and workability are just right. She becomes involved with serious digging, then leaves some moisture or cat fertilizer. The little feline sniffs, as all cats do, and goes through the motion of covering up,

In the meantime I have moved to other sites and other weeds. As soon as she has finished her activity, Blondie hurries to accompany me once more. My inspector is back on the job.

ET CETERA
And Others of the Like Kind

DOGGONE IT

Chasing cars was the joy of our fat dog;
All the neighbors said, "Watch out for that dog-
   Try to keep him confined,
   He may be struck behind,
And your fat dog will wind up a flat dog."

DOG DAYS

   There once was a canine named Rover,
   Didn't listen when told to roll over.
      But when out for play,
      Liked rolling in hay,
   And over and over in clover.

THE DIVINE ESSENCE

There is in all living things, an essence
Of immortality;
Intangible, indestructible;
An element, incapable of being synthesized
By non-God creatures.

There is in all living things, a force,
The intelligence of its kind;
Ever evolving as life is in evolution;
Born of one Creator,
In a stream of endless miracles.

There is in all living things, a soul,
The essence of immortality.

VISIT TO THE VET

This morning I woke up and purred;
You stroked me–I enjoy
Attention, so I meowed–
"Nice cat," you said, "good boy.'

My head felt strange and hot and light;
I didn't want to eat;
My paw looked big, I didn't care-
A cat can use three feet.

And suddenly, this afternoon,
You put me in a crate,
And then you took me, bumpty-bump-
I couldn't know my fate.

You took me to a building,
No attention to my plight;
You let a stranger pick me up
And hold me awfully tight.

He stuck me then with something sharp,
Which added to my pain.
My paw was hurting badly, so
I hissed and clawed–in vain.

He did some nasty things to me,
And you stood calmly by;
I couldn't fight or get away-
All I could do was cry.

Again inside the box, and home;
You said, "good pussy cat."
So why the aggravation, please?
Why did you do all that?

CAT CHRISTMAS

This morning Billy woke me up
And pushed me off the bed.
"It's Christmas, Jeannie," he called out,
"And Tabby, come," he said.

The boy and girl raced down the stairs.
I followed, close behind.
All week I heard that Christmas word–
I wondered what I'd find.

"Look, Santa Claus came here last night
And brought us lots of toys."
I jumped on all the packages;
They made a crackly noise.

"Stop, Tabby, get away from here–
Go find some place to play.
We want to open presents
And right now you're in the way."

They hurt my feelings. I lay down
Behind the strange new tree.
I thought I'd watch them while I hid
And see what I could see.

"A train," said Billy happily,
And Jeannie hugged a bear.
I saw no present for a cat;
I meowed–it wasn't fair.

"Oh, come out, Tabby," Billy called.
"There's something here for you."
I crawled out through those piles of wraps.
I had a package too!

They tore the paper off my gift-
My toy, a catnip mouse.
I danced around it for a while,
Then chased it through the house.

Soon both their Mom and Dad came down
And gave my head a pat.
Then they and we had lots of food.
I am a lucky cat!

SCAREDY CAT

Scaredy cat, scaredy cat, what bo you do?
"I hide from everyone, even from you."
Scaredy cat, scaredy cat, where have you been?
"Under the car, where I couldn't be seen."

Scaredy cat, scaredy cat, I understand;
I offer friendship, come sniff my hand.
"You offer friendship, fine from afar,
"But I think I'll stay here under the car."

THE FELINE

He's lean and grey; he stalks a prey;
Not his is the decision-
So swift of paw, so sharp of claw,
His hearing keen—and vision.

He has no choice; he had no voice-
His species designated
To hunt and kill; the thought or will
Not his—but so created.

NO JUSTICE

You gave me something round and soft
And said, "Go play with that."
It didn't move or anything–
No interest to a cat.

I went outside and something moved;
I had to make it stop.
It even made a little sound;
I watched and saw it hop.

I pounced and it still moved a bit;
I watched–I don't know why.
It made a little sound again;
I pounced–then you came by.

"Bad boy," you said, and grabbed my nape
For no apparent cause.
"Let go that lizard," you then said;
I opened wide my claws.

You took away from me my toy
And, in the house, for fun
You gave me that round stupid thing
That wouldn't squirm or run.

It isn't fair; you bullied me;
You're bigger and you're strong.
I did what any cat would do
And what you did was wrong.

Why didn't you go out and look
And find yourself a toy
Instead of stealing, taking mine–
And calling _me_ "bad boy."?

FRED AND WILLIE

Fred G. had a cat who was healthy and male;
He loved that young tom from his nose to his tail.
"I'll not have him "neutered," declared Mr. G.
"He should have a sex drive like you and like me."

The cat's name was Willie (and sometimes called "Will");
Like all other tomcats, he couldn't be still;
At night, he would roam and would fight with his kin.
He'd always get beaten but never give in.

He didn't find females, but couldn't stay home;
He had to keep looking, for God made him roam
Across busy highways and into strange drives;
He nearly was killed, losing eight of his lives.

He still found no females, what route he would try;
His ears both were torn, and he had one good eye;
His tail became broken from all his fierce fights,
Or maybe by people he kept awake nights.

Each time he was hurt, he was sent to the vet
To be sutured and pilled–what a fate for a pet!
The vet said, "Now, listen, I'll give you advice;
You know I like patients, but this one's too nice

"To be punished–you see what he's faced;
The next time you'll lose him. Too bad, what a waste!
If you have him neutered, he'll be more at ease;
He won't be so frightened–for fun he'll climb trees.

"He'll stay near the house and be happy and purr–
And wait till you see the new shine on his fur!
And more than that, Fred, we're prolonging his life;
I'm surprised that he's living–with all of that strife.

"And Fred, he's a cat, not a person; you see
That he is not you, and that you are not he.
So you have success in your search for a mate.
But, Fred, have him neutered before it's too late."

TO A CAT

When I do something you can't do,
    Like opening a door,
I wonder, sometimes, seeing you,
    If you've had lives before.

When I see how you watch my hand,
    Attentive and alert,
I wonder if you understand
    And if, somehow you're hurt.

When I see reason in your eyes
    And wisdom in your face,
I wonder then, if you despise
    The stupid human race.

WHY DO I LOVE YOU?

Why do I love you, little cat,
Little animal?

Because you come to me with trust,
Seeking nurturance,

With a rub and a purr
And a chirp.

And you follow at my feet.

Why do I love you, little cat,
Little animal?

Because you make me become
My best—

You call forth my kindness, my tenderness,
My gentleness,

The protection for the weak and the helpless
By the strong.

Without you, I am mere mortal—
Stumbling, afraid.

In your eyes, I am reflected as a god.

SEPARATE AND UNEQUAL

I hear them calling me a dog-
I know I am a cat.
Of course, I am a little large-
There's nothing wrong with that.

The ones they call the cats are in
The house; its's clean and dry,
And I am tied up in the yard;
I sit and wonder why.

I have a place that's just for me-
My doghouse, I was told.
It's hot and humid summertime,
And wintertime, it's cold.

Through doors of glass I look inside
And see them eat and play;
I don't know why I am alone-
A separate me and they.

"Good dog," you say when you're with me.
I talk—it does sound strange.
I wonder why the other cats
Speak in a different range.

"Oh, he won't bite," you say to friends,
"A pussycat, that's Spot."
I should be with the other cats;
Please tell me why I'm not.

WILD KITTEN ADOPTED

You picked me up—I thought I'd fall;
I struggled hard to get away.
You are so big, and I'm so small;
I jumped—I was afraid to stay.

I don't know how I now am here;
I used to run with outside cats.
We looked at those like you in fear
And ducked to miss your "pets" and "pats."

Then I knew hunger but was free,
And now there's more than I can eat;
You missed the others, but caught me;
Still you advance, and I retreat.

I see your other cats come by;
You pet them, and they stretch and purr.
I try to hide—sometimes I cry-
But now and then you stroke my fur.

It feels so good I'm not that scared;
I come out to be petted. Then
I purr, but wonder how I dared
Approach you, and I hide again.

I can't get out, I can't go back
To have my freedom; it is lost.
I'm never hungry, never lack-
But with my fear, I think, what cost!

You giant, how would you respond
If you were I and I were you?
Would you then trust, could you be fond
Of bears and tigers, lions too?

TIPPED SCALES

Today, at lunch, I overheard
Two ladies talk about a bird
A neighbor's cat had killed.

Their indignation made it plain
They sympathized with bird in pain
And mourned its song, now stilled.

The waiter brought their food; I saw
Two plates with chicken, fries and slaw
And some assorted dips.

I watched them tear into each bird
That someone killed, and yet no word
Of slaughter left their lips.

They tore apart the limbs, sucked bone-
(Had this bird lived; had this bird flown?)
Their mouths were rimmed with fat.

They were not bothered in the least
That their enjoyment was the feast
They had begrudged the cat.

BIBLIOGRAPHY

(Books with evidence of animal survival)

Barbanell, Sylvia, When Your Animal Dies. London: Spiritualist Press, 1961.

Canfield, Jack, et al, Chicken Soup for the Cat & Dog Lover's Soul. Deerfield Beach, FL: Health Communications, Inc., 1999. (Angie's Dog Always)

Fitzpatrick, Sonya. What the Animals Tell Me. New York: Hyperion, 1997. (Chapter 12)

Holzer, Hans. Dixie Ghosts. Norfolk, VA: The Donning Company, Publishers, 1990. (Oklahoma)

Kowalski, Gary. The Souls of Animals. Walpole, NH: Stillpoint Publishing. 1991.

Moore, Joyce Elson. Haunt Hunter's Guide to Florida. Sarasota, FL: Pineapple Press. 1998. (Shell Mound at Cedar Key)

The Reader's Digest Association, Inc. Mysteries of the Unexplained. Pleasantville, NY: Reader's Digest, 1992. (Spectral Incursions–the Frozen Fowl of Pond Square, The Major's Revenge)

Roberts, Mary. Animal Ghost Stories. Little Rock, AR: August House, Inc. 1995.

Terhune, Albert Payson (Anice). Across the Line. New York: E.P. Dutton. 1961.

Van Praagh, James. Talking to Heaven. New York: Dutton, The Penguin Group. 1997. (Charlie)

INDEX OF TITLES

ALMOST A DOG	12
ANOTHER CAT TALE	96
* ANYBODY WANT A DOG?	27
BEWILDERED MITTY	102
BLACKIE	50
BLONDIE AND FRIEND	102
BLONDIE AND THE CARS	101
BLONDIE OUTSIDE	98
CANDY	30
* CANINE COMMUNICATION	79
* CAT CHRISTMAS	107
CAT CIRCUS	66
CAT JERRY	51
* CHOW TIME	48
CONFRONTATION AT THE "C" CORRAL	37
* DAILY ROUTINE	21
* DIVINE ESSENCE, THE	105
* DOG DAYS	105
* DOGGONE IT	105
EIGHT THAT WALK, THE	71
* EQUAL, BUT SEPARATE	19
EXIT WHITEY	81
FAREWELL, LONESOME	88
* FELINE CHOW TIME	26
* FELINE, THE	108
* FRED AND WILLIE	110
FROM THE BEGINNING	1
FUN AND GAMES	52
* FURRY FUN	73
GARAGE CATS AND THE MILK, THE	85
* GONE	29
* GREENER GRASS	16
HE-ERE'S JOHNNY	60
INDIVIDUALS	34
INSPECTOR, THE	104
INSTINCTS	94
INTRODUCTION, THE CENTRAL ISLIP YEARS	9
INTRODUCTION, THE ORLANDO YEARS	17
JAMIE	53
JERRY'S MORNING	46
* JINNY	42
JINNY JOINS US	39
JINNY'S DAY	75

JINNY'S QUANDARY	84
LONESOME	22
LONESOME AND THE VISITOR	49
* MITTY SPEAKS	80
MITTY'S DILEMMA	95
MITTY'S ORDEAL	92
* NANCY AND BLACKIE	13
* NO JUSTICE	109
* NOBODY'S DOG	21
* OLD CAT SYLVIE	28
* ON THE DEATH OF CURLY, A FAVORITE PET	20
* QUINTET	78
RANDY'S TOY	103
RUSTY AND LONESOME	63
SAY "CHEESE"	44
* SCAREDY CAT	108
* SEPARATE AND UNEQUAL	113
* SHERRY	16
SICK CAT	86
SPAT	85
TALE OF CLAWS, A	76
TAMING BLONDIE	74
* TIMMY	14
* TIPPED SCALES	115
* TO A CAT	111
* UNIQUE	57
* VISIT TO THE VET	106
* WALKING OUR DOG ON AN EARLY SPRING MORNING	83
WATCHING MITTY	91
* WHY DO I LOVE YOU?.	112
* WILD KITTEN ADOPTED	114
WILLY	7
WOOGA-WOOGA	58
YOUNG AND THE AGELESS, THE	43

* Poetry

INDEX OF FIRST LINES, POEMS

A stray kitten, barely returned to life 57
Animals are all unique, though lion, dog, or mouse. 19
Big cat Blackie was curled up and sleeping 13
Blackie gets impatient, so he gives the rest a cuff 26
Chasing cars was the joy of our fat dog 105
"Come on, Sylvie, time to eat 21
Fred G. had a cat who was healthy and male 110
He is gone 29
He was Shere Khan, my baby cat, Sherry 16
He's lean and grey; he stalks a prey 108
I hear them calling me a dog 113
I never cease to be amazed 79
If Johnny eats from that one bowl 80
In the morning, when I walk him, he decides to scratch and sit 27
It is still dark, pre-dawn 83
Johnny chases Jinny 78
Our Jinny is an elf, a sprite 42
Our Jinny jumps into my lap 73
Scaredy cat, scaredy cat, what do you do 108
Some carpeting is Jerry's toy 51
The neighborhood adored him 14
There is in all living things, an essence 105
There once was a canine named Rover 105
This morning Billy woke me up 107
This morning I woke up and purred 106
Today, at lunch, I overheard 115
When I do something you can't do 111
When you are inside the house 16
While cleaning house 28
Why did you die, my little cat 20
Why do I love you, little cat 112
You gave me something round and soft 109
You picked me up–I thought I'd fall 114
You shared our lives a few short weeks 21

ABOUT THE AUTHOR

Ida Riman was born in Toledo, Ohio, in 1921, lived in Freeport, New York, through her twenties, and in New York City for a number of years. She majored in art in high school and was a technical illustrator for over 30 years. On one job, working for a publications firm in New York City, she met and later married Joseph Percoco.

She studied nights and earned a BA in English in 1969 and a MS in library science in 1971. For a few years she was a librarian. She set up the library and catalogued the books at the Suffolk Marine Museum in West Sayville, New York. After moving to Orlando, Florida, in 1978, she worked as a technical illustrator for over two years, then became a real estate saleswoman and broker.

She has always written on all topics. Many of her poems and prose articles have been published. In this volume, she shares her experiences--the joys and heartaches of a pet owner.

She is also the author of a book of short poems (1994), LIMERICKS AND MINI-POEMS and a chapbook (1997), A IS FOR ANIMAL B IS FOR BIRD.